T3-BHN-268

BAKELAND

BAKELAND

Nordic Treats Inspired by Nature

MARIT HOVLAND

foreword by

TRINE HAHNEMANN

GREYSTONE BOOKS
Vancouver/Berkeley

CONTENTS

FOREWORD

I am a keen baker of cakes and breads. I've been baking since childhood, and have a special love of home baking. I'm not a trained pastry chef, but learned by doing. Before I knew I was going to be a chef, I was a stay-at-home mom to my small children for some years. Baking was part of our everyday life, and I would bake cakes more than once a week. For special occasions my children and I would make theme cakes using our imaginations and various homemade decorations. Since I didn't know any techniques, I discovered everything through trial and error. *Bakeland* by Marit Hovland would have been my dream book.

When I first read *Bakeland*, I was mesmerized by all the amazing ideas Marit brings to life. She finds ways to bring nature into the kitchen, combining home baking with artful but nonprofessional decorating using natural ingredients. She lives up to a basic rule of mine: don't use anything your grandmother wouldn't recognize as food.

The recipes are relatively easy. Some are a little more complicated than others, but all can be accomplished by anybody with a passion for baking. Just read the recipes before you start, then follow the instructions carefully, and you will go on a journey with Marit that is fun and creative.

Marit's inventions bring cake and cookie decorating down to earth without compromising on aesthetics or on flavor. Imagination is a big part of this baking book. I love the little meringue mushrooms, the green coconut Christmas trees, the strawberry macarons, the icing butterflies, and the cookies that look like birches—iconic trees here in the North.

The recipes are well tested and they work. I baked from the book with great joy together with my ten-year-old niece Mathilde, who also loves *Bakeland*. We've flipped through it numerous times and have a list of things we still want to make—treats to look forward to for every season.

Bakeland celebrates Nordic life in the way it is structured around the seasons. Seasons are very important in the Nordic countries. They define our everyday life. The light tells us which month we are in and what time of day, and we eat and live accordingly. Produce comes and goes with the seasons, which may be very short: berries are only in season for six to eight weeks, so we eat them every day while they last.

I love the way that light plays into these recipes, offering inspiration in terms of patterns and ideas—for example, the cookies with small clouds. Some of the decorations even have interesting echoes of Nordic painters.

Seasons are also about cold and warm temperatures. We tend to eat heavier things in winter than in summer; we need sweet things to get us through the dark winter months, and summer cakes to celebrate the light and the more welcoming weather.

I think we need a world in which more baking takes place at home, rather than just being something we watch chefs do on television. This book should be used regularly in the kitchen, its pages getting dusted with flour and spotted with icing. It could bring families together on a Saturday for a baking project. Or it could inspire a baking-themed birthday party, where the children bake the cake themselves.

Or you could just spend a day baking all by yourself, and your dream cake will come to life. I promise it is the best and most stress-free time you can have. For myself, when the world is running too fast, I go into my kitchen and bake a cake. Marit Hovland's *Bakeland* has inspired new ideas that I am excited to explore. I recommend this book to anybody who bakes.

Bake with love,

Trine Hahnemann
Author of *The Scandinavian Cookbook* and *Scandinavian Baking*

HI!

It's nice of you to come along to Bakeland, a place I hope and believe you'll enjoy.

I am neither a professional baker nor a pastry maker, but I have always loved to bake, and the kitchen has been my playground since I was little. It's a place where I can relax, have fun, and be creative.

As a child growing up in Norway, I was always welcome in the kitchen, both as a helper and to experiment on my own. It didn't matter if the kitchen was covered in flour from floor to ceiling when I was done—creative messes were always welcome in my home! Over the years, I put my mixing bowls and measuring spoons to good use as I explored my curiosity, tackled new tasks, and learned new things.

I'm excited to have the opportunity to share my recipes with you, whether you're a skilled pastry chef already or someone who enjoys baking for fun. What you're holding in your hands is my very first book, a collection of baking recipes that I can truly call my own. Everything in it is mine: the original idea, the photos, and the recipes. As a professional graphic designer, I was determined from the start to take on the design and layout of the book myself.

Inspiration can be found everywhere. I always carry a notebook wherever I go—I recommend it. You never know when ideas will pop into your head. For this book, I have been inspired by all things beautiful in nature. I always say that I have four favorite seasons: winter, spring, summer, and fall. With my recipes, I invite you to come along on a splendid, tasty trip through an entire year of Norwegian nature!

In Norway, every season is beautiful, each in its own way. Winter, with its intricate snowflakes and ice crystals; spring, when everything in nature is reborn; summer, with its spectacular sunsets and fields of abundant wildflowers; and fall, the season of glowing colors and crisp air. Whichever part of the world you live in, you'll find beauty in the changing moods and colors of the seasons. If you keep your eyes open when you're out walking, you may notice—and revel in—tiny details you've never paid attention to before.

I have tried to use techniques and instructions in this book that anyone can follow. For many of the recipes, there are step-by-step illustrations, which show that although at first glance the desserts may seem advanced, they're actually relatively simple. With a few tips and tricks, anyone can be an artistic baker.

My decorations can be simplified, made more advanced, or ignored completely. Maybe you have some favorite baking recipes that you could dress up using suggestions from this book? Or maybe it will provide you with entirely new ideas? All the more fun, if that's the case.

Even though I love decorating my baking, taste has always been my first priority. I use a lot of fruits, nuts, berries, and spices in my recipes, and I want everything to taste as tempting as it looks. After all, it's meant to be eaten and enjoyed. For that reason, I avoid using too much food coloring, and you won't find much use for fondants here.

I'm dedicated to finding solutions that don't require a kitchen full of specialty tools. Most techniques can be accomplished using items you already have at home: aluminum foil, toothpicks, cotton swabs, and regular paper.

I hope this book will inspire you to try new things in the kitchen. The joy and sense of achievement you feel when you step outside your comfort zone are underrated. Regardless of whether the result is flawless, you'll end up feeling proud once you've made the first attempt. And when it comes to baking, it's hard to render the result inedible! Don't give up too soon—as with most things in life, practice makes perfect. I've learned a lot through trial and error.

You'll find recipes here for various kinds of sweets: cakes, cookies, yeast breads, macarons, and confections—something for every taste. I take my cues from nature in Norway, and the traditions and flavors I know. You can easily adapt my ideas to nature where you are, and to traditions and flavors you're familiar with. Or you can let yourself be inspired by my northern ways.

I look forward to seeing what you bake! If you're so inclined, share your photos with me on Instagram. You can find me under the name @borrowmyeyes.

Finally, happy baking—and have fun!

Marit

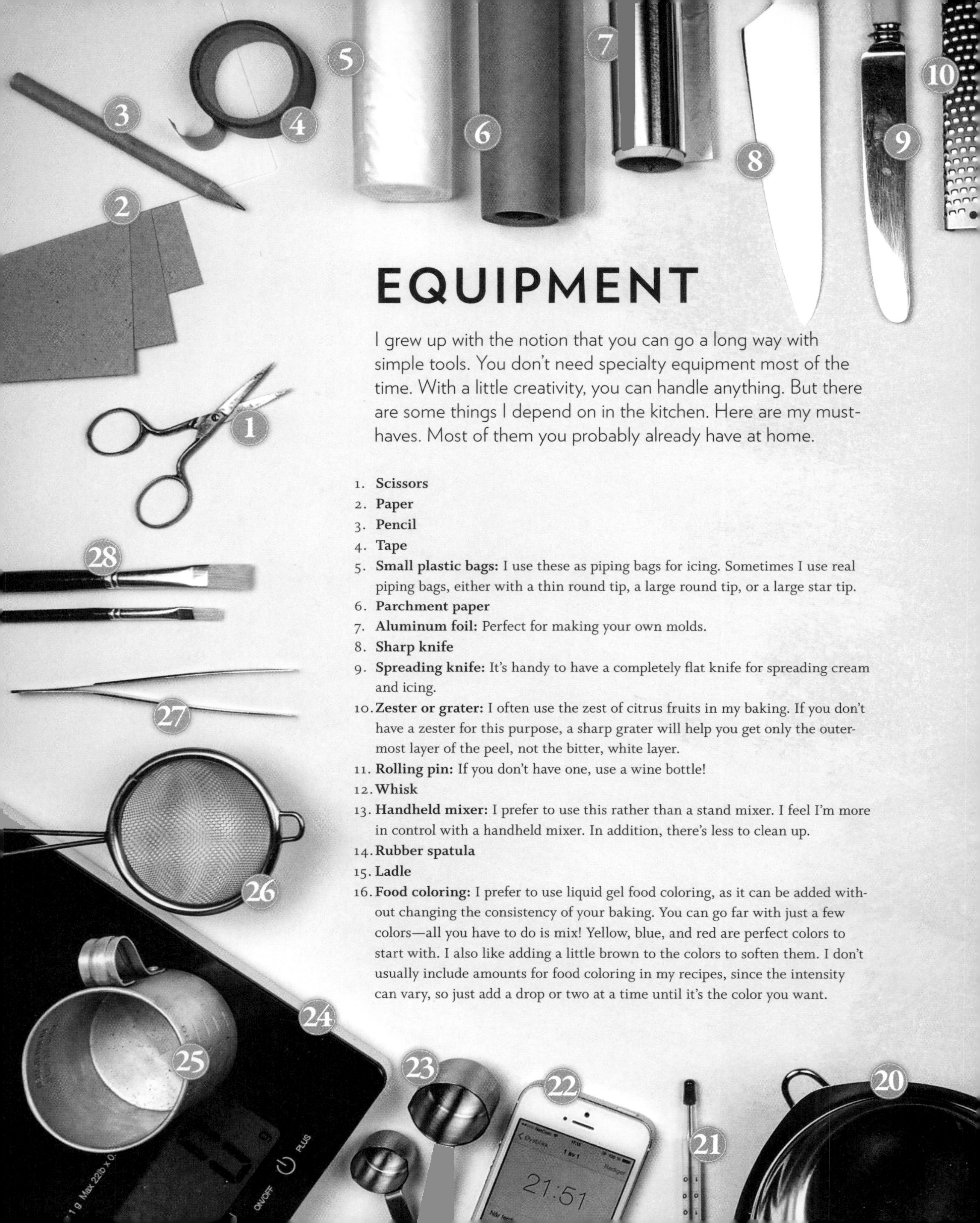

EQUIPMENT

I grew up with the notion that you can go a long way with simple tools. You don't need specialty equipment most of the time. With a little creativity, you can handle anything. But there are some things I depend on in the kitchen. Here are my must-haves. Most of them you probably already have at home.

1. **Scissors**
2. **Paper**
3. **Pencil**
4. **Tape**
5. **Small plastic bags:** I use these as piping bags for icing. Sometimes I use real piping bags, either with a thin round tip, a large round tip, or a large star tip.
6. **Parchment paper**
7. **Aluminum foil:** Perfect for making your own molds.
8. **Sharp knife**
9. **Spreading knife:** It's handy to have a completely flat knife for spreading cream and icing.
10. **Zester or grater:** I often use the zest of citrus fruits in my baking. If you don't have a zester for this purpose, a sharp grater will help you get only the outermost layer of the peel, not the bitter, white layer.
11. **Rolling pin:** If you don't have one, use a wine bottle!
12. **Whisk**
13. **Handheld mixer:** I prefer to use this rather than a stand mixer. I feel I'm more in control with a handheld mixer. In addition, there's less to clean up.
14. **Rubber spatula**
15. **Ladle**
16. **Food coloring:** I prefer to use liquid gel food coloring, as it can be added without changing the consistency of your baking. You can go far with just a few colors—all you have to do is mix! Yellow, blue, and red are perfect colors to start with. I also like adding a little brown to the colors to soften them. I don't usually include amounts for food coloring in my recipes, since the intensity can vary, so just add a drop or two at a time until it's the color you want.

17. **Springform pan:** I bake all my round cakes in the same pan. Nice and simple! All the recipes fit a pan with a diameter of 9 inches (23 cm).
18. **Toothpicks:** Good for so many things: adding liquid gel food coloring, making holes, testing cakes . . .
19. **Muffin pan:** You can bake cupcakes in liners without a pan, but using a muffin pan allows you to pour more batter into the cups and get higher cupcakes.
20. **Stainless steel bowl:** To heat ingredients over hot water, if you don't have a double boiler pot. Perfect for melting chocolate, heating up lemon cream, etc.
21. **Candy thermometer:** Cooking with both sugar and chocolate is so much easier with a thermometer.
22. **Timer**
23. **Measuring spoons:** Use proper measuring spoons rather than a regular teaspoon or tablespoon, which can vary in size. With measuring spoons, you'll get the same result each time.
24. **Scale:** It is important to me to have a scale that I can reset with contents on it. This makes it easier to add ingredients to your bowl.
25. **Measuring cups:** I've provided cup measurements in these recipes alongside weight measurements (in grams). If you do have a kitchen scale, weighing your solid ingredients (flour, sugar, nuts, etc.) will give you a more precise amount.
26. **Tea strainer:** I often sift icing sugar and cocoa powder over my baking through a tea strainer. Macarons, on the other hand, require a bigger flour sifter.
27. **Tweezers:** To make it easier to position decorations, for example, or to remove something that has ended up in the wrong place.
28. **Brush:** Useful for brushing off things you don't want on your baking, and for painting on color, cocoa powder, egg white, and other things.
29. **Large cake pan (not pictured):** For larger cakes, I use a rectangular baking pan measuring 12" × 16" (30 × 40 cm). You could also use a lasagna pan.
30. **Nut grinder (not pictured):** Essential for grinding nuts finely for marzipan—otherwise the dough will be difficult to handle. For chopping nuts, you can either chop by hand or pulse in a food processor.

WINTER INTO SPRING

The snow melts away as the mercury rises. You can hear the melting water trickle, forming little creeks. Nature slowly awakens after the long winter. The first flowers show their heads, and the trees are budding. Everything that was brown now turns to bright shades of green.

MACARONS WITH PASSION FRUIT CREAM

makes 35 macarons

Spring is here! The Norwegian coltsfoot flower is impatient. Before the snow has even disappeared, its yellow bristly head pops out of the dirt, brightening roadsides and ditches. Macarons with a refreshing passion fruit filling are the perfect way to welcome spring.

Macarons

¾ cup + 2 Tbsp (85 g) almond flour
¾ cup + 2 Tbsp (110 g) icing sugar
2 medium egg whites (70 g)
pinch of salt
3 Tbsp (35 g) granulated sugar

Sift the almond flour into a bowl. Stir in the icing sugar, then sift again into another bowl.

Using a handheld mixer, beat the egg whites at medium speed until foamy. Add the salt. Gradually add the sugar, continuing to beat at medium speed. When all of the sugar has dissolved and you have a thick meringue, fold in the almond flour mixture with a rubber spatula. When the mixture is smooth, transfer it to a piping bag.

Pipe out the macarons onto a macaron baking mat or a baking sheet lined with parchment paper, forming circles about 1¼ inches (3.5 cm) in diameter (you can use the template on page 198). Tap the baking sheet with the macarons once against the kitchen counter so any big air bubbles rise to the surface and burst.

Preheat the oven to 250°F (125°C) on the convection setting, or 275°F (135°C) on the regular setting. Allow the macarons to dry for about 40 minutes on the counter, then bake them on the middle rack of the oven for 15 minutes, or a few minutes longer if you're using the regular oven setting. See page 190 for more detailed instructions.

Passion fruit cream

2 passion fruits
2 egg yolks, whisked
⅓ cup (70 g) granulated sugar
2 Tbsp (30 g) butter, cut into cubes and kept cold

Cut the passion fruits in half and scoop out the flesh, then press it through a strainer to make juice.

Combine 2 Tbsp (30 ml) of the passion fruit juice with the egg yolks and sugar in a double boiler, or directly in a saucepan over low heat. Heat, stirring constantly. When the mixture starts to thicken, remove it from the heat and stir in the butter. Set aside to cool.

Decoration

yellow liquid gel food coloring
water
1 egg white
1 tsp lemon juice
approximately 1⅔ cups (200 g) icing sugar

In a small bowl, mix a few drops of food coloring with a little water. Using a small brush, draw lines from the middle of the macaron shell to the edge to make flower petals. Repeat this on half of the shells.

Make icing with the egg white, lemon juice, and icing sugar according to the instructions on page 188. Add a few drops of yellow food coloring. Transfer to a piping bag. Make a small hole and pipe out little dots into the middle of each of the decorated macarons. Sandwich the macarons together with the passion fruit cream, using a plain macaron on the bottom and a decorated one on top. Keep in the refrigerator until you're ready to serve.

COFFEE ICE CREAM CAKE WITH CHOCOLATE MERINGUE

makes one 9-inch (23 cm) round cake

The sun has melted most of the snow on the mountain, and you can finally hike to the top again. Dramatic chocolate meringue mountains decorate this coffee ice cream cake with a crispy meringue crust. The cake is easy to make, but it does take some time in the oven and the freezer, so make it a day ahead.

Chocolate meringue

- 3 medium egg whites (100 g)
- pinch of salt
- ¾ cup + 2 Tbsp (180 g) granulated sugar
- 2½ Tbsp unsweetened cocoa powder, divided

Preheat the oven to 175°F (75°C) on the convection setting, or 200°F (90°C) on the regular setting. Using a handheld mixer, beat the egg whites at medium speed until foamy. Add the salt (which makes the meringue firmer). Gradually add the sugar, continuing to beat at medium speed until the sugar is dissolved and you have a thick meringue. Using a rubber spatula, gently fold in 2 Tbsp of the cocoa powder.

Fill a piping bag with a little less than half of the mixture. Cut a fairly large hole or use a large round tip. Pipe out mountains onto parchment paper by squeezing and pulling upward. Sift ½ Tbsp of cocoa powder through a tea strainer onto the meringue mountains. Spread the rest of the meringue evenly in the bottom of a 9-inch (23 cm) round springform pan lined with parchment paper. Put both the pan and the baking sheet with the mountains in the oven and leave the meringues to dry for about 5 hours. Remove from the oven and cool.

Coffee ice cream

- 3 egg yolks
- ¾ cup (140 g) granulated sugar
- 2 Tbsp strong coffee, cooled
- 1¼ cups (300 ml) whipping cream
- ¼ tsp vanilla bean seeds, or 1 tsp vanilla sugar or extract

Using a handheld mixer, beat the egg yolks and sugar together until pale in color. Gently stir in the cooled coffee. In a separate bowl, whip the cream until fluffy using a handheld mixer. Add the vanilla seeds toward the end. Gently fold the egg mixture into the whipped cream. Spread the mixture over the meringue in the pan. Cover the pan with plastic wrap or aluminum foil and put the cake in the freezer overnight.

Decoration

- 1 oz (30 g) bittersweet baking chocolate, chopped or grated
- icing sugar

Remove the cake from the freezer 10 minutes before serving. While it thaws, sprinkle the chocolate over the cake and place the meringue mountains on top. Finally, sift some icing sugar to dust the mountaintops with snow.

Variations: For a more child-friendly version, skip the coffee in the ice cream. Nuts and pieces of chocolate can also be added to the ice cream. You can make the meringue without cocoa as well.

COCONUT OATMEAL COOKIES

makes 30 cookies

The white anemone, poking its head through the wilted leaves, is yet another sign of spring in Norway. In some places, the entire forest floor is covered in a white carpet. Mini marshmallows, cut diagonally, form the sweet white anemones on these chewy cookies.

Oatmeal cookies

- ½ cup (110 g) butter, at room temperature
- ½ cup (100 g) granulated sugar
- ½ cup (100 g) brown sugar
- 1 egg
- 1 cup (125 g) all-purpose flour
- 1 cup (100 g) quick-cooking oats
- ⅓ cup (35 g) unsweetened shredded coconut
- ½ tsp salt

Preheat the oven to 375°F (190°C). Line a baking sheet with parchment paper.

In a mixing bowl, whip the butter and sugars together with a whisk until fluffy. Add the egg and whisk well. Stir together the remaining ingredients in a separate bowl, then add them to the butter mixture and stir until combined.

Roll the dough into little balls, approximately 2 tsp each. Flatten them a little on the baking sheet. Bake the cookies for 8 to 10 minutes on the middle rack of the oven. Transfer them to a wire rack to cool.

White anemones

- 1 egg white
- 1 tsp lemon juice
- approximately 1⅔ cups (200 g) icing sugar
- green liquid gel food coloring
- 90 small marshmallows
- small gold sugar pearls

Make the icing with the egg white, lemon juice, and icing sugar according to the instructions on page 188. Put half of the mixture into a piping bag. Add some food coloring to the rest of the icing to make it green, adding a drop or two at a time until it's the color you want, then fill another piping bag.

Follow the instructions on page 23 to decorate the cookies. Store them in an airtight container.

Variation: Add chopped dried fruit, nuts, or chocolate to the cookie dough.

1
2
3
4
5
6

1. Cut the marshmallows diagonally from one flat end to the other. Each marshmallow will make 2 petals. **2.** Pipe a spot of white icing in the middle of the cookie. **3.** Place 6 petals, flat side down, in a circle on the icing. Repeat with the rest of the cookies. **4.** Pipe a dot of green icing in the middle of the flower. **5.** Place gold sugar pearls around the edge of the green dot while it's still wet. **6.** Also place a gold sugar pearl at the base of each petal. It will stick in the marshmallow.

God påske

CHOCOLATE ALMOND COOKIE EGGS

makes 25 cookies

The birds are chirping, and you can tell they're happy spring is here. Siskins lay especially pretty eggs—white or light blue with brown speckles. I make the spots on these egg-shaped cookies with the help of a toothbrush and some cocoa powder. Covered in lemon icing, they're just right for the season.

Almond cookies
1¾ cups (250 g) almonds
1⅔ cups (200 g) icing sugar
1 Tbsp all-purpose flour
zest of 1 lemon
1 egg white
2 Tbsp lemon juice

Preheat the oven to 350°F (180°C). Line a baking sheet with parchment paper.

Grind the almonds in a nut grinder. In a bowl, stir together the ground almonds, icing sugar, flour, and lemon zest. Add the egg white and lemon juice. Using your hands or the dough attachment of a stand mixer, work the dough well until all the ingredients are combined. You'll find instructions on how to shape the egg cookies on the next page.

Bake the cookies for about 8 minutes on the middle rack of the oven. Transfer them to a wire rack to cool.

Chocolate filling
5 oz (150 g) milk chocolate

When you get to step 5 on the next page, temper the chocolate (see page 187). Transfer to a piping bag.

Lemon icing
2 Tbsp lemon juice
1¼ cups (150 g) icing sugar
blue liquid gel food coloring

For step 6, you'll need the lemon icing. In a bowl, stir together the lemon juice and icing sugar. Divide the mixture into two parts and add the blue food coloring to one part, using a drop at a time until it's the color you want.

Spots
1 tsp vanilla extract
1 tsp unsweetened cocoa powder

In a small bowl, stir together the vanilla extract and cocoa for step 7.

These chocolate-filled eggs make perfect Easter gifts. Save an empty egg carton and cover the label with fancy paper. Place a cookie egg in each dimple and tie a ribbon around the carton. Pick a small twig of pussy willows and attach it to the outside along with an Easter card.

1. Copy the egg pattern on page 198 onto a sheet of regular paper. Place a sheet of parchment paper on top. **2.** Roll out little balls (around 2 tsp) of the almond dough. Narrow them at one end so the balls form an egg shape in accordance with the template. Flatten the balls onto the parchment paper so they cover the whole template. Transfer to the prepared baking sheet. **3.** Bake the cookies as instructed on page 25. **4.** Find pairs of cookies that fit together. **5.** Pipe out some chocolate onto one of the cookie bottoms and place the other cookie on top. Don't pipe the chocolate all the way to the edge. When you put on the lid, the chocolate will inevitably be squeezed a little further out. Repeat with the remaining cookies. **6.** Dip one side of each cookie in the lemon icing. Shake it well before you turn it over and set it down to dry for half an hour. Use the white icing for half the cookies and blue for the other half. **7.** Dip a clean toothbrush in the cocoa mixture. Drag your finger over the brush to spray spots onto the cookies. You can also use any other small brush with stiff bristles. **8.** Let the icing harden completely before you put the cookies in an airtight container.

CARDAMOM MACARONS WITH BLUEBERRIES AND CREAM CHEESE

makes 10 large macarons

The bright color of the blue anemone, common in Norway in the spring, is a lovely sight on the otherwise brown forest floor. The petals are usually royal blue or purple, in stark contrast to the chalk-white pistils. Using a potato, you can easily print these pretty blue anemones onto macarons.

Cardamom macarons

¾ cup + 2 Tbsp (85 g) almond flour
¾ cup + 2 Tbsp (110 g) icing sugar
1 tsp ground cardamom
2 medium egg whites (70 g)
pinch of salt
3 Tbsp (35 g) granulated sugar

Sift the almond flour into a bowl and stir in the icing sugar and cardamom. Sift again into another bowl.

In a separate bowl, using a handheld mixer, beat the egg white at medium speed until foamy. Add the salt. Gradually add the sugar, continuing to beat at medium speed. When the sugar has dissolved and you have a thick meringue, add the almond flour mixture and use a rubber spatula to beat it into the meringue. When the mixture is smooth, transfer it to a piping bag.

Pipe out the macarons onto a macaron baking mat or a baking sheet lined with parchment paper, forming 2¼-inch (6 cm) circles (use the template on page 198). Tap the baking sheet with the macarons once against the counter so any big air bubbles rise to the surface and burst. Let the macarons dry for about 40 minutes on the counter.

Preheat the oven to 250°F (125°C) on the convection setting, or 275°F (135°C) on the regular setting. Bake the macarons for 15 minutes in the middle of the oven (if you're using a regular oven they may take a few minutes longer). Remove and cool. For more detailed instructions, see page 190.

Decoration

1 potato
purple or blue liquid gel food coloring
water
icing sugar

While the macarons are drying and baking, you can get ready to decorate. Follow the instructions on page 31.

Filling

⅓ cup (75 g) plain cream cheese
1½ cups (175 g) icing sugar
zest of 1 lemon
½ Tbsp lemon juice
1¼ cups (170 g) blueberries

In a bowl, stir together the cream cheese, icing sugar, lemon zest, and juice. Transfer to a piping bag and pipe the filling onto half of the macaron shells. Place a circle of blueberries around the edge of each macaron before you top with the lid. Keep the macarons in the refrigerator until ready to serve.

1. Copy the blue anemone patterns on page 198 onto a sheet of paper. 2. Cut out the flowers. 3. Halve a potato. With a sewing pin, fasten a paper flower to each half. 4. Use a sharp knife to cut away the potato around the flower. 5. Remove the paper and pins. 6. Mix a few drops of food coloring with some water. Paint the color onto the potato flower with a brush. 7. Gently press the potato against the macaron shell. Make as many flowers as you like on each shell. If you press the potato several times without adding more color, you'll get varying shades of blue in the flowers. 8. Dip a brush in a little icing sugar and tap it gently in the middle of each flower to make pistils.

APRICOT COCONUT CHOCOLATE CAKE

makes one large baking pan

Covered in green coconut grass and white anemones made from puffed rice, this cake will remind your guests of spring. The apricot filling makes the cake extra moist.

Puffed rice white anemones

1 egg white
1 tsp lemon juice
approximately 1⅔ cups (200 g) icing sugar
green liquid gel food coloring
puffed rice
small gold sugar pearls

Follow the instructions on page 188 to make icing with the egg white, lemon juice, and icing sugar. Scoop out a little of the icing into a separate bowl and stir in a few drops of green food coloring. Put the white icing in one piping bag and the green icing in another. Follow the instructions on page 35 to make the flowers.

Chocolate cake

⅔ cup (150 g) butter
4.5 oz (130 g) bittersweet baking chocolate, coarsely chopped
4 eggs
1¼ cups (250 g) granulated sugar
1 cup (250 ml) buttermilk
3 Tbsp strong coffee
2¼ cups (270 g) all-purpose flour
3 Tbsp unsweetened cocoa powder
4 tsp baking powder

Preheat the oven to 350°F (180°C). Line a large baking pan or lasagna pan (around 12" × 16"/30 × 40 cm) with parchment paper.

In a saucepan over medium heat, melt the butter, then remove from the heat. Stir the chocolate into the hot butter until it melts. While the mixture is cooling, using a handheld mixer, beat the eggs and sugar together in a bowl until pale in color. On low speed, beat in the chocolate mixture, buttermilk, and coffee.

Stir together the flour, cocoa powder, and baking powder in a separate bowl. Sift the dry ingredients into the batter and fold in with a rubber spatula. Pour the batter into the prepared baking pan and bake the cake on the middle rack of the oven for about 15 minutes. Test the cake by sticking a toothpick into the middle. If it comes out clean, the cake is done.

Place the pan on a wire rack to cool for 10 minutes, then loosen the cake and turn it out on the rack to cool completely.

Filling and icing

⅓ cup (100 g) apricot jam
1 tsp water
green liquid gel food coloring
⅓ cup (30 g) unsweetened shredded coconut
2 Tbsp (25 g) butter, melted
¾ cup (100 g) icing sugar
½ Tbsp unsweetened cocoa powder
2 Tbsp strong coffee

When the cake is cool, slice it horizontally to make two layers. Spread the apricot jam on one layer, then place the other layer on top.

Preheat the oven to 350°F (180°C). In a small bowl, mix 1 tsp of water with a few drops of food coloring. Add the shredded coconut and stir to coat. Spread the coconut on a baking sheet covered in parchment paper. Place it in the preheated oven to dry for about 2 minutes.

In a small bowl, stir together the melted butter, icing sugar, cocoa, and coffee. Spread the icing over the cake, reserving a little to stick on the flowers, then sprinkle on the dried shredded coconut. Place the flowers on top, gluing them on with some icing if needed.

1. For each flower, you'll need 6 rice puffs. Try to find puffs of the same size. 2. On a sheet of parchment paper, pipe out a spot of the white icing. Place 2 rice puffs opposite each other with one end in the icing. If you study the puffs carefully, you will see a notch on one side. Make sure the notch of each rice puff is pointing toward the middle—then they will fit together like puzzle pieces. Put the final 4 rice puffs in place. 3. Pipe a small dot of green icing in the middle. 4. If you want to make pistils, you can place some gold sugar pearls around the green dot. 5. Let the flowers dry for at least 15 minutes. The longer they dry, the more handling they can withstand. Store the flowers in an airtight container. They can be kept for several months.

BIRCH BARK COOKIES

makes 22 cookies

Birch trees are easily recognizable from their characteristic white bark. As the trees grow older, the glossy bark cracks and forms dark furrows. Surprise your guests with these crisp birch bark cookies made with the classic combination of vanilla and chocolate.

Vanilla cookies

⅔ cup (150 g) butter, at room temperature
⅔ cup (125 g) granulated sugar
1 egg
2 cups (250 g) all-purpose flour
½ tsp baking powder
¼ tsp vanilla bean seeds, or 1 tsp vanilla sugar

Preheat the oven to 400°F (200°C). Line a baking sheet with parchment paper.

Using a handheld mixer, whip the butter and the sugar together in a bowl until fluffy. Add the egg and mix well.

In a separate bowl, stir together the flour, baking powder, and vanilla seeds or sugar. With the mixer on low speed, beat the flour mixture into the butter mixture until combined.

For each cookie, take around 1½ Tbsp of dough and form it into a sausage shape, the thickness of your finger. Flatten slightly onto the prepared baking sheet. The cookies should be around ⅛ inch thick (3 to 5 mm). Bake the cookies for 8 to 10 minutes on the middle rack of the oven. Transfer them to a wire rack to cool.

Decoration

3.5 oz (100 g) bittersweet baking chocolate
1 egg white
1½ cups (190 g) icing sugar
2 Oreo cookies

Follow the instructions for the decorations on page 39.

Remove the white filling from the Oreo cookies, put the cookies in a plastic bag, and crush them with a rolling pin.

1
2
3
4
5
6
7
8

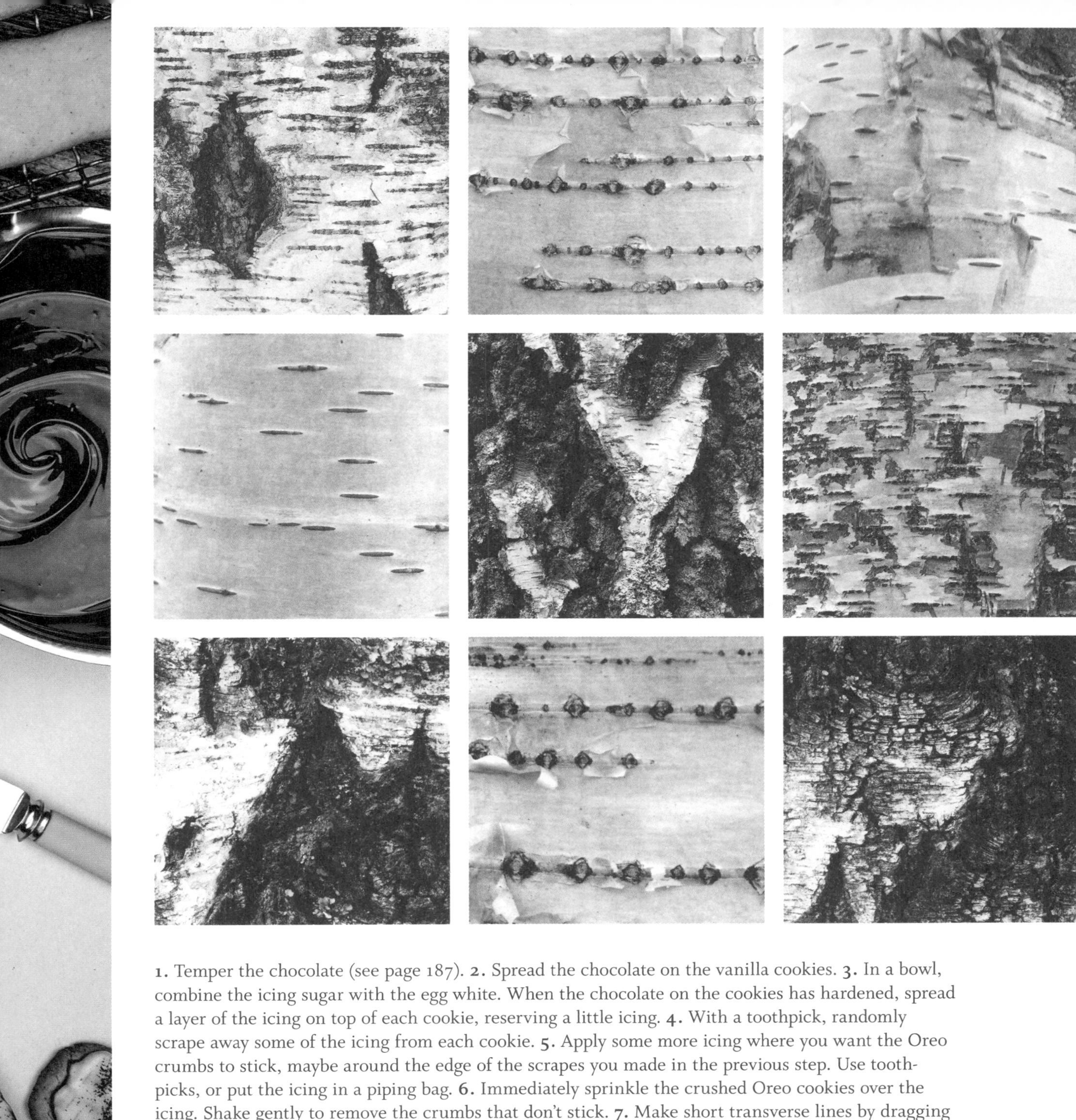

1. Temper the chocolate (see page 187). **2.** Spread the chocolate on the vanilla cookies. **3.** In a bowl, combine the icing sugar with the egg white. When the chocolate on the cookies has hardened, spread a layer of the icing on top of each cookie, reserving a little icing. **4.** With a toothpick, randomly scrape away some of the icing from each cookie. **5.** Apply some more icing where you want the Oreo crumbs to stick, maybe around the edge of the scrapes you made in the previous step. Use toothpicks, or put the icing in a piping bag. **6.** Immediately sprinkle the crushed Oreo cookies over the icing. Shake gently to remove the crumbs that don't stick. **7.** Make short transverse lines by dragging a sharp knife across the white icing. **8.** Now the cookies are ready to be eaten or to be stored in an airtight container.

Variation: A simpler alternative to the decoration is to spread icing on the cookies first, then put the tempered chocolate in a piping bag and draw stripes on the cookies.

CHOCOLATE ROCKS WITH FRUIT AND NUT FILLING

makes 100 chocolate rocks

Stones that have been rocked back and forth by waves at the water's edge become smooth, and feel soft to the touch. These chocolate rocks, filled with nuts and dried fruit, look just like the real thing, but are much tastier!

Chocolate shells

2 Oreo cookies
7 oz (200 g) white chocolate, chopped
6 Tbsp (90 ml) sweetened condensed milk
pinch of salt
⅛ tsp unsweetened cocoa powder

Crush the Oreo cookies by removing the white filling, placing the cookies in a plastic bag, and using a rolling pin.

In a saucepan over low heat, combine the chocolate, condensed milk, and salt, stirring constantly. Remove the saucepan from the heat as soon as the mixture is smooth. Stir in half of the crushed Oreo cookies.

Follow the instructions on the next page to shape the rocks.

Filling

¼ cup (30 g) salted peanuts
¼ cup (30 g) salted cashews
2 Tbsp (20 g) dried sweetened cranberries

Follow the instructions for the filling on the next page. You can also make chocolate rocks without a filling, but the white chocolate on its own is very sweet. You can substitute other kinds of nuts and dried fruit as well.

Tip: Use the rocks as decoration on a cake—maybe the chocolate cake on page 33 or the nut cake on page 105.

1. Divide the white chocolate mixture evenly into 3 small bowls. Leave bowl 1 as is. For bowl 2, stir in the rest of the crushed Oreo cookies. For the last bowl, stir in the cocoa powder. **2.** Cover the bowls with plastic wrap or aluminum foil. Let them stand at room temperature for 30 minutes. **3.** Place a sheet of parchment paper on a pastry board and lay out the nuts and cranberries. **4.** Scoop out a small piece of one of the chocolate mixtures and flatten it. Place a nut or a cranberry in the middle and press it in. Roll the chocolate with your hands so it takes the shape of a rock. Repeat with the remaining chocolate mixtures, nuts, and cranberries. **5.** Leave the rocks on parchment paper to harden for a few hours at room temperature. **6.** Store the rocks in an airtight container until you're ready to serve them.

1
2
3
4
5
6

MINT-GLAZED HAZELNUT COOKIES

makes 18 cookies

Look up! Maybe you'll see an interesting cloud in the sky today. Clouds soar by in all shapes and sizes. Allow your imagination to soar along with them and decorate these soft hazelnut cookies in cloud patterns with the help of a kitchen sponge.

Hazelnut cookies
1½ cups (250 g) hazelnuts
1⅔ cups (200 g) icing sugar
1 Tbsp all-purpose flour
1 egg white
1 Tbsp lemon juice

Preheat the oven to 350°F (180°C). Line a baking sheet with parchment paper.

Grind the hazelnuts using a nut grinder. In a bowl, combine the ground hazelnuts with the icing sugar and flour. Add the egg white and lemon juice. Work the dough well with your hands until the ingredients are combined.

Dust some icing sugar on your pastry board and roll out the dough with a rolling pin until it is approximately ¼ inch (7 mm) thick. Cut the dough into approximately 2-inch (5 cm) squares, or use cookie cutters. Transfer to the prepared baking sheet and bake for 10 minutes on the middle rack of the oven. Transfer the cookies to a wire rack to cool.

Mint glaze
1 egg white
2 tsp lemon juice
approximately 1⅔ cups (200 g) icing sugar
few drops peppermint oil

In a bowl, stir together the egg white, lemon juice, and icing sugar. Add peppermint oil to taste—it's very strong, so add just a little at a time! Transfer to a piping bag.

Decoration
blue liquid gel food coloring
water

Mix a few drops of food coloring with a little water. For further instructions, see page 47.

Tip: A great way to roll out an even dough is to find two items of the same height you want your dough (here, ¼ inch/7 mm)—for example two pieces of wood, or two magazines or books. Place these on either side of the dough so that the rolling pin rolls on them. That way, the dough will be the same thickness all the way across.

1
2
3
4
5

1. Apply the glaze to the cooled cookies. It works best to draw the outline of the glaze first, then fill in the middle. Let the glaze dry for a couple of hours before you make the clouds. The longer you let it dry, the less careful you have to be with the sponge. 2. Cut a new, clean kitchen sponge into small pieces. Make sure to use a natural sponge, not an antibacterial one, as they contain harmful chemicals. 3. Dip the sponge in the food coloring mixture. Press it a couple of times on a piece of paper to get rid of some of the liquid in the sponge before you apply it to the cookies. 4. Gently press the sponge on the cookies. 5. You can also drag the sponge across the glaze to make stripes. Store the cookies in an airtight container.

SPRING INTO SUMMER

The days are long, and the evening sun gives off a lovely, warm glow. Sunbeams set off sparkles in the water. Forests and fields abound with flowers in all the colors of the world. Juicy berries begin to ripen everywhere. Summer is a time for refreshing flavors.

LEMON POPPY SEED CUPCAKES

makes 18 cupcakes

"Look, a brimstone butterfly! That means summer is here!" I remember reading in a book when I was a child. Have you ever seen a butterfly roll out its portable straw and suck up the nectar? Say hello to summer with these refreshing and moist lemon cupcakes.

Butterflies

1 egg white
1 tsp lemon juice
approximately 1⅔ cups (200 g) icing sugar
yellow liquid gel food coloring

Start by making the icing butterflies. They need time to dry, preferably overnight. Follow the instructions on page 188 to make icing with the egg white, lemon juice, and icing sugar, adding a few drops of yellow food coloring. Follow the instructions on the next page to shape the butterflies.

Lemon cupcakes

½ cup (100 g) butter, at room temperature
1 cup (200 g) granulated sugar
3 eggs
1⅔ cups (200 g) all-purpose flour
2 tsp baking powder
½ tsp salt
zest of 2 lemons
⅔ cup (150 ml) lemon juice
¼ cup (30 g) poppy seeds

Preheat the oven to 350°F (175°C). Line two 12-cup muffin pans with 18 liners (leave the rest of the cups empty).

Using a handheld mixer, whip the butter and sugar together in a bowl until fluffy. Add the eggs one at a time, mixing well after each one.

In a separate bowl, stir together the flour, baking powder, and salt. Sift this into the egg mixture and fold it in with a rubber spatula. Stir in the lemon zest, juice, and poppy seeds. Fill the muffin cups and bake for about 20 minutes on the middle rack of the oven.

Syrup

juice of ½ lemon
3 Tbsp (35 g) granulated sugar

While the cupcakes are baking, make the syrup. In a saucepan, bring the lemon juice and sugar to a boil. When the sugar has dissolved, remove from the heat. Brush the cupcakes with the syrup while they are still lukewarm. This will keep them moist.

Icing

2 Tbsp lemon juice
approximately 1 cup (125 g) icing sugar

In a bowl, stir together the lemon juice and icing sugar. Spread over the cupcakes and fasten a butterfly in the icing before it hardens.

Variation: Use other citrus fruits to vary the cupcakes. If you want to make the cupcake liners yourself, see page 194.

1
2
3
4
5

1. Copy the butterfly shapes on page 198 onto a sheet of paper. 2. Place the drawings of the butterflies under a sheet of parchment paper. You can fasten the parchment paper with tape to keep it in place. Put the yellow icing in a piping bag and pipe icing along the outline of one of the upper wings before you fill in the rest. Repeat with the opposite wing. Then do the same with the lower wings. 3. When the wings are dry, loosen them from the paper. 4. Fold a piece of parchment paper in half and put it in an open book. Pipe a line of icing in the fold. Attach the wings to each side of the line. 5. When the butterflies are dry, loosen them from the paper. They will keep for several months in an airtight container.

WHITE CHOCOLATE LIME CAKE WITH ALMONDS

makes one 9-inch (23 cm) round cake

Forget-me-not. The name itself is as charming as the tiny, sky-blue flower. This is a refreshing summer version of the popular chocolate brownie cake, featuring white chocolate and lime and decorated with sliced almonds and candied forget-me-nots.

Forget-me-nots
forget-me-not flowers
1 egg white
pinch of salt
superfine granulated sugar

Start by making the candied forget-me-nots, following the instructions on page 57.

Lime cake
5 oz (150 g) white chocolate, finely chopped
1 cup (200 g) granulated sugar
¼ cup (60 ml) lime juice
zest of 1½ limes
2 eggs
⅓ cup (90 g) butter
1½ cups (185 g) all-purpose flour
¼ tsp salt

½ cup (70 g) sliced almonds

Preheat the oven to 350°F (175°C). Line the bottom of a 9-inch (23 cm) round springform pan with parchment paper.

Place the chocolate in a mixing bowl. In a separate bowl, whisk together the sugar, lime juice, lime zest, and eggs.

In a saucepan, melt the butter, then pour over the chocolate and stir. When the chocolate has melted, add it to the egg mixture.

In a separate bowl, combine the flour and salt. Sift the dry ingredients into the batter and fold in with a spatula.

Pour the batter into the prepared pan and sprinkle the sliced almonds on top. Bake for 25 to 30 minutes on the middle rack of the oven. Let the cake cool, then decorate with candied forget-me-nots. The cake should be kept in the refrigerator until you're ready to serve it.

Tip: If you're not in the mood to pick the flowers—or it's the wrong time of year—you can make icing forget-me-nots. Follow the instructions on page 61, but use blue and yellow food coloring.

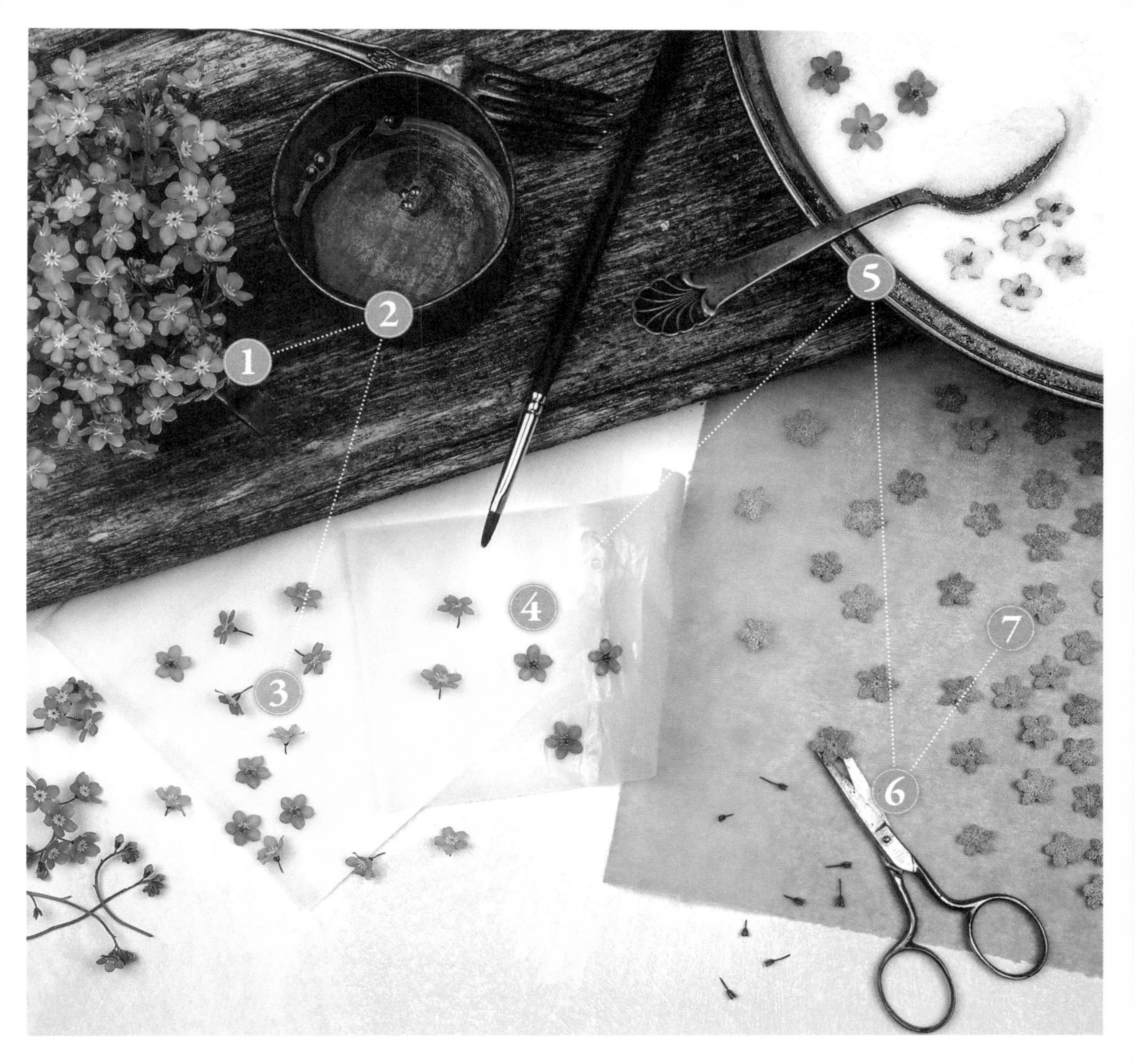

1. Go for a walk and pick a bouquet of forget-me-nots. **2.** With a fork, lightly whisk an egg white with a pinch of salt. **3.** Pinch off the flower, leaving a small part of the stem attached. It's easier to hold the tiny flower this way. **4.** Use a small brush to gently paint both the back and the front of the flower with egg white. I usually lay a piece of parchment paper under the flower. When too much egg white has ended up on the paper, I simply exchange it for a new piece. **5.** Sprinkle the whole flower with superfine granulated sugar and gently shake off the excess. **6.** Cut off the last little piece of the stem. **7.** Let the flowers dry, right side up, on parchment paper. They will dry fairly quickly, but let them rest overnight if possible. The candied flowers can be kept for several months in an airtight container.

SESAME–GINGER BUNS WITH LEMON ICING

makes 12 buns

Can you see the yellow glow when you hold a buttercup flower under your chin? If so, you'll probably love these buns, filled with butter, sesame seeds, and ginger. They're extra tasty topped with a bright lemon icing.

Buttercups
1 egg white
1 tsp lemon juice
1⅔ cups (200 g) icing sugar
yellow and green liquid gel food coloring
superfine granulated sugar

Start by making the buttercups. Make icing with the egg white, lemon juice, and icing sugar according to the instructions on page 188. Scoop out one third of the icing into a separate bowl. Color the remaining two thirds of the icing yellow, and the smaller amount green, adding a drop or two of food coloring at a time until the icing is the color you want. On page 61, you'll find instructions for shaping the buttercups.

Buns
¼ cup (65 g) butter, melted
1 cup (250 ml) whole milk
3 Tbsp (25 g) fresh yeast, or 1½ Tbsp (12 g) active dry yeast
4 cups (500 g) all-purpose flour
⅓ cup (80 g) granulated sugar
1 tsp ground cardamom
½ tsp salt
1 egg yolk

In a mixing bowl, stir together the melted butter and milk. When the mixture is lukewarm, crumble the yeast into the bowl.

In a separate bowl, stir together the flour, sugar, cardamom, and salt. Add the dry ingredients to the yeast mixture, then add the egg yolk. Work the dough with your hands to combine, kneading for about 10 minutes. Cover the bowl with plastic wrap and let it rise for about 50 minutes.

Filling and decoration
3½ Tbsp (50 g) butter, at room temperature
1 Tbsp ground ginger
3 Tbsp (40 g) granulated sugar
3 Tbsp (40 g) sesame seeds

1 egg white
pearl sugar, coarse sugar, or crushed sugar cubes
sesame seeds

⅔ cup (75 g) icing sugar
3 tsp lemon juice

Stir together the butter, ginger, sugar, and sesame seeds in a bowl.

When the dough has risen, gently knead it on a floured pastry board. With a rolling pin, roll out the dough into a square. Spread the filling on the square, leaving a ½-inch (1 cm) clean edge along one side. Begin rolling from the side opposite the clean side. Brush some egg white on the clean edge before sealing. Using a sharp knife, slice the roll in pieces about ¾ inch (2 cm) wide. Line two baking sheets with parchment paper. Place the buns on the baking sheets, cover with a clean kitchen towel, and let them rise again for about 30 minutes.

Preheat the oven to 425°F (225°C). Brush the buns with egg white and sprinkle them with pearl sugar and sesame seeds right before you bake them on the middle rack of the oven for 8 to 10 minutes. Remove and transfer them to a wire rack to cool.

In a bowl, stir together the icing sugar and lemon juice. Spread on the cooled buns. Place buttercups in the icing.

1
2
3
4
5
6
7
8
9

1. Pipe out dots of green icing on parchment paper. Make some dots big, others small. These will be the centers of the flowers. 2. Sprinkle the dots with superfine granulated sugar while they're still wet. The sugar will stick and provide texture. 3. When the dots have dried, put them in a strainer and shake to remove excess sugar. 4. Trace the star pattern on page 198 onto a piece of paper. This will help you make all the petals the same size and position them correctly. 5. Place a sheet of parchment paper over your drawings. You can tape it to the table so it doesn't shift. 6. Place a green icing dot in the middle of each pattern. 7. Pipe out yellow icing dots all around. You can place the opening of the piping bag on the thick line and pipe until the dot meets up with the thin lines on either side. Then you'll know the petal is big enough and that there's room for 5 petals of the same size. 8. Wait for a few minutes before you pipe out the petals next to each other. Then continue until all are done. 9. Leave the flowers to rest overnight. The drying time depends on the moisture in the icing and the temperature in the room. When the flowers have dried, remove them from the parchment paper. They can be kept for several months in an airtight container.

CHOCOLATE CAKE WITH PASSION FRUIT FILLING

makes one 9-inch (23 cm) round cake

The violet flower ranges in color from the dark of night to the light of day. This moist, layered chocolate cake, filled with tart passion fruit syrup, makes the perfect backdrop for a wreath of violets in a field of nuts.

Candied violets
night-and-day flowers
1 egg white
pinch of salt
superfine granulated sugar

Start by making the candied flowers, following the instructions on page 65. Night-and-day is a type of violet. All violets are edible and can be candied.

Chocolate cake
½ cup (115 g) butter
3.5 oz (100 g) bittersweet baking chocolate, coarsely chopped
3 eggs
1 cup (190 g) granulated sugar
¾ cup (175 ml) buttermilk
3 Tbsp coffee
1⅔ cups (200 g) all-purpose flour
2 Tbsp unsweetened cocoa powder
3 tsp baking powder

Preheat the oven to 350°F (180°C). Line the bottom of a 9-inch (23 cm) round springform pan with parchment paper.

In a saucepan, melt the butter, then remove from the heat. Add the chocolate and stir until it melts. While the chocolate mixture cools, using a handheld mixer, beat together the eggs and sugar in a bowl. On low speed, beat in the chocolate mixture, buttermilk, and coffee.

In a separate bowl, stir together the flour, cocoa powder, and baking powder. Sift the dry ingredients into the batter and fold in.

Pour the batter into the prepared pan and bake for about 35 minutes. To test the cake, stick a toothpick into the middle—if it comes out clean, the cake is ready. Let it cool completely before you slice it horizontally into three layers.

Passion fruit syrup
5 passion fruits
½ cup (100 g) granulated sugar

Halve the passion fruits and scoop out the flesh, then press it through a strainer. Measure out ½ cup (125 ml) of the juice. Combine the juice and sugar in a saucepan and bring to a boil over medium heat. Let simmer for 5 minutes, stirring constantly. Remove from the heat and let it cool.

Spread half of the syrup on the bottom layer of the cake.

Buttercream
½ cup (100 g) butter, at room temperature
1⅔ cups (200 g) icing sugar
1½ Tbsp buttermilk

Using a handheld mixer, whip the butter and icing sugar together until fluffy. When you're almost there, add the buttermilk. Spread the buttercream on top of the cake and down the sides. This makes enough for a thin layer of icing. Double the ingredients if you want the icing to cover the whole cake.

Decoration
⅓ cup (50 g) pistachios, chopped

Sprinkle the nuts on the cake and decorate with the flowers.

1. Go for a walk and pick night-and-day violets. Put them in water until you're ready to use them. **2.** With a fork, whisk the egg white lightly with a pinch of salt. **3.** Pinch off the flower about 1 inch (2.5 cm) down the stem so you have something to hold on to. Hold the flower with your fingers and paint egg white on the top side. Lay down the flower and paint the back side. I prefer to put them on parchment paper, which is easy to replace when it gets messy. **4.** Dip the flower in the sugar, front side down. Sprinkle sugar over the back side with a spoon. **5.** Lift the flower out of the sugar by the stem. Gently shake off excess sugar so that only a thin layer remains. Let the flower dry. If you prefer a flat flower, lay it front side down. If you want a more natural-looking flower, lay it back side down. Cut off the stem. **6.** Let the flowers dry. They dry fairly quickly, but let them rest overnight if possible. The flowers can be kept for several months if stored in an airtight container.

WHITE CHOCOLATE SEASHELLS WITH RASPBERRY FILLING

makes 20 chocolate seashells

Wade barefoot at water's edge, smell the sea air, and listen to the sound of the lapping waves. Summer is here! Bring home a couple of shells and—as if by magic—you'll have lifelike chocolate seashells with the help of some aluminum foil.

Raspberry filling 1½ cups (200 g) raspberries (thawed if frozen) ½ cup (100 g) granulated sugar	Press the raspberries through a strainer to get rid of the seeds. Put the mashed raspberries and sugar in a saucepan and bring to a boil over medium heat. Let the mixture simmer for 10 minutes, without a lid, stirring constantly. Remove from the heat and let it cool.
Chocolate seashells 7 oz (200 g) white chocolate	Follow the instructions on page 69 to make the seashells.

Variation: If you can find salt licorice syrup, you can add it to the raspberry filling for an authentic Scandinavian flavor. You can also fill the chocolate shells with other kinds of berries, nougat, nuts, or caramel.

1
2
3
4
5
6
7
8

1. Take a walk on the beach and gather some shells. Try to find a few of different sizes. **2.** Cut out sheets of aluminum foil quite a bit larger than the seashells. Place a sheet of foil over a seashell and use your fingers to rub the foil into the shell. Make sure to rub the top side so you get the texture of the seashell. **3.** Place a glass upside down on the aluminum foil seashell. Fold up the edges. **4.** Turn the glass, and right there you will have a mold. The real seashell is now free to be used for the next mold. Each mold can only be used once. Make as many as you wish. **5.** Temper the chocolate (see page 187). Pour a little chocolate into the mold and turn the glass so the chocolate covers the shell. You don't need to fill the whole space—just make a shell. **6.** When the chocolate has hardened, add the raspberry filling. Leave some room to seal the shell with chocolate. **7.** Finally, cover the shell with chocolate. **8.** When the chocolate has hardened, the aluminum foil can easily be lifted off the glass and removed from the chocolate. Keep the chocolate seashells at room temperature. If it's warm, you may want to keep them in the refrigerator.

CARDAMOM BUNS WITH ALMOND FILLING

makes 16 buns

If you look closely at a wild rose petal, you'll notice that it has the shape of a heart. The lovely simplicity and fragile appearance of a white or blush wild rose contrasts with the thorns of the woody branches. Decorate these romantic-looking buns with candied wild roses.

Wild roses

16 wild roses
1 egg white (for roses)
pinch of salt
superfine granulated sugar
1 egg white (for icing)
1 tsp lemon juice
approximately 1⅔ cups (200 g) icing sugar
yellow liquid gel food coloring
small gold sugar pearls

On page 73, you'll find the instructions for making candied wild roses. Make them the day before you want to use them.

You will need yellow icing to assemble the candied roses. Follow the instructions on page 188 for making icing with the egg white, lemon juice, and icing sugar. Use a few drops of food coloring to color the icing yellow.

Buns

¼ cup (65 g) butter, melted
1 cup (250 ml) whole milk
3 Tbsp (25 g) fresh yeast, or 1½ Tbsp (12 g) active dry yeast
4 cups (500 g) all-purpose flour
⅓ cup (80 g) granulated sugar
2 tsp ground cardamom
½ tsp salt
1 egg yolk
1 egg, for brushing (optional)

Almond filling

¾ cup (100 g) almonds, finely chopped
⅔ cup (75 g) icing sugar
1 egg white
1 tsp rum extract

Combine the melted butter and milk in a mixing bowl. When the mixture is lukewarm, crumble the yeast into it.

In another bowl, stir together the flour, sugar, cardamom, and salt. Add to the yeast mixture, then add the egg yolk. Work the dough with your hands for about 10 minutes. Cover the bowl with plastic wrap and let the dough rise for 50 minutes.

In a bowl, combine the almonds, icing sugar, egg white, and rum extract.

Knead the risen dough lightly and divide it into 16 pieces. Flatten each bun slightly, put a heaped teaspoon of the almond filling in the middle, and close the bun like a bag. Turn the bun so that the seam is facing down and roll it into a bun shape. Repeat with the rest of the pieces of dough. Place the buns on two baking sheets lined with parchment paper. Cover them with clean kitchen towels and let them rise again for about 30 minutes.

Preheat the oven to 425°F (225°C). If you want the buns to be glossy, whisk an egg lightly with a fork and brush the buns before baking. Bake for 7 to 9 minutes in the middle of the oven. Transfer the buns to a wire rack to cool.

Decoration

icing sugar (optional)

Sprinkle some icing sugar over the buns. Pipe out some icing to fasten the flowers.

2
4
5
3
6

Go for a walk and pick wild roses. If you're going to use them immediately when you get home, take only the flowers or the petals. If not, include the stem and put them in water until you need them. You can also use garden roses or roses from the florist, as long as they haven't been sprayed.

With a fork, whisk an egg white with a pinch of salt. Disassemble the flowers and paint both sides of the petals with the egg white. Cover both sides of the petals with superfine granulated sugar and let them dry on parchment paper.

1. Get a couple of glasses and aluminum foil. This is not necessary, but it will make it easier to assemble the roses again. Put foil across the glass and gently press down so you have a little dip. **2.** Pipe a spot of icing in the bottom of the foil dip. Place a petal there. **3.** Continue with the remaining 4 petals. Let them slightly overlap. **4.** Pipe out a small dot of icing in the middle of the flower and sprinkle with a little superfine sugar. **5.** When the flowers have dried, you can remove them from their foil forms. If you want pistils, you can use the same icing as before to make a tiny circle around the yellow dot in the middle of the rose. Sprinkle with sugar pearls. Remove the excess pearls. **6.** The flowers can be kept for several months in an airtight container.

ROSEMARY CUPCAKES WITH LEMON CREAM

makes 12 cupcakes

Is there anyone who hasn't picked a daisy, pulled out petal after petal, and asked: "Loves me, loves me not?" I think you'll love these rosemary cupcakes, filled with a tart lemon cream and topped with a daisy made of icing sugar.

Lemon cream

2 Tbsp (30 g) butter
2 egg yolks
⅓ cup (70 g) granulated sugar
2 Tbsp (30 ml) lemon juice

Cut the butter into cubes and keep them cold. Put all the ingredients, except the butter, into a double boiler, or a stainless steel bowl over a saucepan with water, and heat, stirring constantly. (You can also put the ingredients directly into the saucepan if you keep it on low heat.) When the mixture begins to thicken, remove it from the heat and stir in the butter. Set aside.

Rosemary cupcakes

¼ cup (65 g) butter, at room temperature
⅔ cup (135 g) granulated sugar
2 eggs
¾ cup (165 g) light sour cream
1 cup (135 g) all-purpose flour
1 tsp baking powder
pinch of salt
1½ tsp dried rosemary

Preheat the oven to 350°F (180°C). Line a 12-cup muffin pan with cupcake liners, or place the liners directly on a baking sheet.

Using a handheld mixer, whip the butter and the sugar together in a bowl until fluffy. Keep whipping while you add the eggs, one at a time, mixing well between each. Fold in the sour cream with a rubber spatula.

In a separate bowl, stir together the flour, baking powder, and salt. Sift the dry ingredients into the wet mixture and fold in. Finally, fold in the rosemary, crushing it a little between your fingers before you add it.

Fill the cupcake liners evenly with the batter. If you're not using a muffin pan, you'll need to use more than 12 liners and fill each one only ⅔ full so it doesn't overflow. You'll also need to reduce the baking time by a few minutes.

Bake the cupcakes on the middle rack of the oven for about 20 minutes. Remove them to a wire rack to cool.

Decoration

icing sugar

On page 77, you'll find instructions for decorating the cupcakes.

1. While the cupcakes are cooling, make the stencil. Copy the daisy pattern on page 200 onto a piece of paper, or draw your own. Cut out the daisy. 2. Use an apple corer to make a hole, approximately 1 inch (2.5 cm) deep, in the middle of each cupcake. 3. Place the stencil on the cupcake so the hole is in the middle of the flower. Sprinkle icing sugar onto the cupcake through a tea strainer. Carefully lift the stencil off the cupcake. Repeat with the remaining cupcakes. 4. Fill a piping bag with the lemon cream and pipe it into the hole on each cupcake. Heap the lemon cream so it makes a raised dot in the center of the flower.

CINNAMON BUN CAKE WITH RUM GLAZE

makes one round bun cake, approximately 10 in (25 cm)

This bun cake is shaped like a daisy because of the special way you cut and twist the dough. The zesty glaze makes this cake the perfect accompaniment to a fine summer's day.

Buns
3½ Tbsp (50 g) butter, melted
⅔ cup (150 ml) whole milk
3 Tbsp (25 g) fresh yeast, or 1½ Tbsp (12 g) active dry yeast
2½ cups (300 g) all-purpose flour
⅓ cup (75 g) granulated sugar
1½ tsp ground cardamom
½ tsp salt
1 egg (for brushing)

Cinnamon filling
2½ Tbsp (35 g) butter, at room temperature
3 Tbsp (40 g) granulated sugar
1 Tbsp cinnamon

Combine the melted butter and milk in a mixing bowl. When the mixture is lukewarm, crumble the yeast into it. In a separate bowl, stir together the flour, sugar, cardamom, and salt, then add to the yeast mixture. Work the dough with your hands for about 10 minutes. Cover the bowl with plastic wrap and let the dough rise for 50 minutes.

Mix together the butter, sugar, and cinnamon in a small bowl.

Knead the dough and divide it into 3 equal parts. Roll each part into a ball. Flatten each ball to a diameter of about 7 inches (17 cm).

Spread half of the filling on one circle, leaving ½ inch (1 cm) clean along the edge. Put the second circle on top and spread the rest of the filling in the same way. Finally, cover with the last circle. Press the edges together. Transfer the bun cake to a baking sheet lined with parchment paper. Press it out to a diameter of about 8 inches (20 cm).

Gently place a glass in the middle of the cake. Use a sharp knife to cut notches from the edge of the cake toward the glass, cutting all the way through the cake to make 16 sections (see page 200). Take hold of one section, gently pulling it from the middle without tearing it. Twist so that the side faces up. Repeat with the rest, twisting each section in the same direction. Let the cake rise again for 30 minutes.

Preheat the oven to 400°F (200°C). Brush the cake with a whisked egg and poke several holes in the middle of the flower with a toothpick. Bake for about 12 minutes on the middle rack of the oven. Transfer the cake to a wire rack to cool.

Rum glaze
1⅔ cups (200 g) icing sugar
1 tsp rum extract
1 Tbsp lemon juice
1½ Tbsp water

In a bowl, stir together the icing sugar, rum extract, lemon juice, and water. Put the mixture in a piping bag and pipe out on the flower petals.

Variation: You can replace the cinnamon filling with a macaron filling. Finely chop ½ cup almonds and mix with ½ cup icing sugar and one small egg white.

WALNUT PAVLOVA WITH WHIPPED CREAM AND BERRIES

makes one 8-inch (22 cm) round cake

In the forest and high up in the mountains, it's not unusual to find large fields of cranesbill geraniums. The flowers are a lovely purple and the leaves change color in the fall. This elegant pavlova says "summer," full of fresh berries and candied cranesbills.

Cranesbills
cranesbill flowers
1 egg white
pinch of salt
superfine granulated sugar

Make the candied cranesbills at least half a day in advance so they have time to dry. Follow the instructions on page 83.

Walnut pavlova
4 egg whites
pinch of salt
1 cup + 2 Tbsp (225 g) granulated sugar
2 tsp cornstarch
1 tsp white wine vinegar
¾ cup (75 g) walnuts, coarsely chopped

Preheat the oven to 350°F (175°C). Line a baking sheet with parchment paper and draw a circle, approximately 8 inches (22 cm) in diameter, on the paper. This will make it easier to form a round cake.

Using a handheld mixer, beat the egg whites in a bowl at medium speed until foamy. Add the salt. Gradually add the sugar, continuing to beat at medium speed until the sugar is dissolved and you have a thick meringue. Add the cornstarch and white wine vinegar, then turn out the meringue onto the prepared baking sheet. Make a dip in the middle of the cake if you want more room for the filling. Sprinkle the walnuts over the cake.

Put the cake in the oven on the middle rack and reduce the temperature to 250°F (125°C). Bake the cake for 75 minutes, then turn off the oven, but leave the cake in until the oven is cold.

Cream and berry filling
1¼ cups (300 ml) whipping cream
2 Tbsp granulated sugar
¼ tsp vanilla bean seeds, or 1 tsp vanilla sugar or extract
¾ cup (100 g) raspberries
¾ cup (100 g) blueberries
¾ cup (100 g) blackberries
¾ cup (100 g) black currants

Using a handheld mixer, whip the cream with the sugar until fluffy. Add the vanilla seeds toward the end. Spread the whipped cream over the pavlova. Decorate with berries and candied cranesbills.

1. Go for a walk and pick cranesbills. Put the flowers in water until you're ready to use them. **2.** Cut strips of paper, approximately ½ inch (1 cm) wide and 3 inches (8 cm) long. **3.** Glue each paper strip into a ring. **4.** Cut the flowers, leaving a bit of the stem so you have something to hold on to. Remove the pistils and the stigma inside the flower. **5.** With a fork, lightly whisk the egg white with a pinch of salt. Paint the front and back of the flower with the egg white. **6.** Dip the flower, front side down, in the sugar. Use a spoon to sprinkle sugar on the back side of the flower. **7.** Cut off the stem. **8.** Set the flower in a paper ring to dry so it keeps its shape.

LIME AND STRAWBERRY MACARONS

makes 18 strawberry macarons and 18 lime macarons

The reason I find little white wild strawberry flowers particularly cute, I think, is because I know they'll turn into such tasty berries. Enjoy your wild strawberries directly from the plant, but use the bigger strawberries to fill these pretty macarons.

Wild strawberry flowers

1 egg white
1 tsp lime juice
approximately 1⅔ cups (200 g) icing sugar
yellow liquid gel food coloring

Make icing with the egg white, lime juice, and icing sugar according to the instructions on page 188. Scoop out half of the icing and add a few drops of yellow food coloring. Put the yellow and white icing in separate piping bags. Pipe out a yellow dot with 5 white dots around it on parchment paper. (See tips on page 61). Let the flowers dry, preferably for a day, before you move them.

Macarons

¾ cup + 2 Tbsp (85 g) almond flour
¾ cup + 2 Tbsp (110 g) icing sugar
2 medium egg whites (70 g)
pinch of salt
3 Tbsp (35 g) granulated sugar
zest of 1 lime
green and red liquid gel food coloring
sesame seeds

Sift the almond flour into a bowl. Stir in the icing sugar, then sift again into another bowl.

In a bowl, using a handheld mixer, beat the egg whites at medium speed until foamy. Add the salt. Gradually add the sugar, continuing to beat at medium speed. When the sugar has dissolved and you have a thick meringue, add the almond flour mixture, using a rubber spatula to beat it into the meringue. When the meringue is smooth, divide it into two bowls. Add the grated lime peel to one, along with some green food coloring. Add red food coloring to the other bowl.

Transfer the mixtures to separate piping bags and pipe out macarons into circle and strawberry shapes, using the patterns on page 198. Sprinkle sesame seeds on the wild strawberry ones. Let the macarons dry for 40 minutes on the counter.

Preheat the oven to 250°F (125°C) on the convection setting, or 275°F (135°C) on the regular setting. Bake for about 15 minutes on the middle rack (a few minutes longer in a regular oven).

Wild strawberry filling

¾ cup (125 g) wild strawberries
3 Tbsp (40 g) granulated sugar
1 tsp fruit pectin powder

Using a handheld blender, puree the strawberries. Put the puree in a saucepan with the sugar and bring to a boil. Reduce the heat and let simmer for 1 minute, then add the pectin. Let it boil for 1 minute, then remove from the heat and allow to cool. Transfer to a piping bag and pipe onto half the red macarons, then top with the other halves.

Cream cheese filling

3½ Tbsp (50 g) plain cream cheese
⅔ cup (80 g) icing sugar

In a bowl, blend together the cream cheese and sugar. Put the mixture in a piping bag and pipe onto half of the green macarons, then sandwich with the other halves. Attach the wild strawberry flowers to the tops with some icing. Keep the macarons in the refrigerator until you're ready to serve them.

SOFT PISTACHIO COOKIES WITH STRAWBERRY GLAZE

20 grass straws

Few things give a Norwegian a stronger feeling of summer than berries on a straw. So find a grass straw or stalk of wheat and thread these little cookies on it instead! The soft pistachio cookies are coated in a real strawberry glaze. They taste good alone, but even better with vanilla ice cream.

Pistachio cookies

- 1½ cups (150 g) unsalted pistachios
- ¾ cup (100 g) almonds
- 1⅔ cups (200 g) icing sugar
- 1 Tbsp all-purpose flour
- 1 egg white
- 1 Tbsp lemon juice
- 20 grass straws

Using a nut grinder, grind the pistachios and almonds into a bowl. Add the icing sugar and flour and stir well.

Add the egg white and lemon juice. Using your hands, work the dough together well. Place it in a plastic bag and keep it in the refrigerator for at least an hour, or preferably overnight. See further instructions on page 89.

Strawberry glaze

- 1¼ cups (200 g) frozen strawberries, thawed
- 1⅔ cups (200 g) icing sugar

This is for step 5 on page 89. Puree the berries using a handheld blender. Put the pureed berries in a saucepan, bring to a boil, and let simmer for approximately 15 minutes, stirring, until reduced by half. Let cool, then stir in the icing sugar.

Tip: If you don't want to pick grass straws, or if you want to create a summer atmosphere in the middle of winter, you can use skewers or simply serve the cookies on their own.

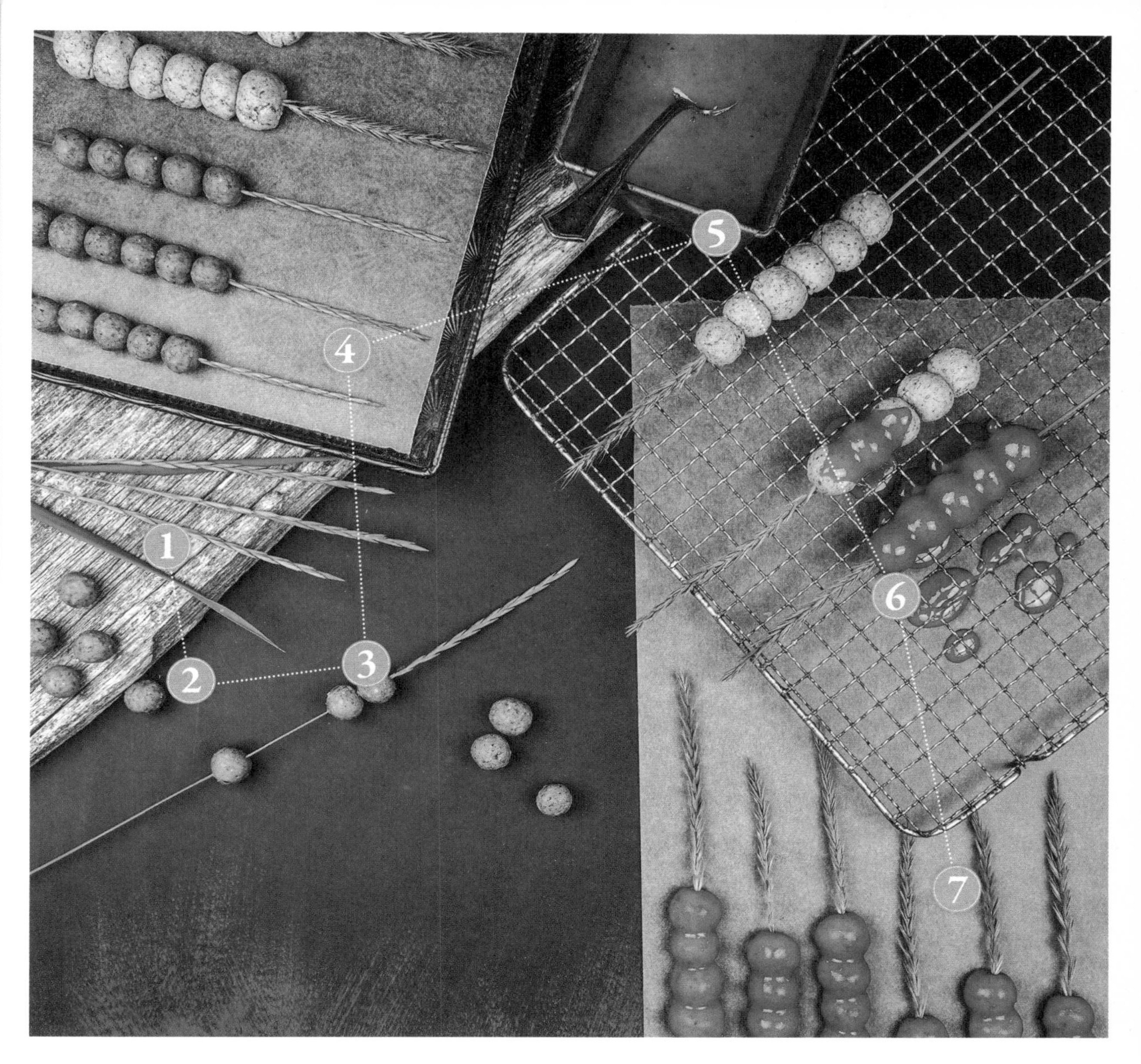

1. Pick grass straws or use skewers. **2.** Preheat the oven to 350°F (180°C) and line a baking sheet with parchment paper. Shape the dough into little balls the size of marbles. **3.** Thread the marbles onto the grass straws. **4.** Lay the cookie straws on the baking sheet. Bake on the middle rack of the oven for 8 to 10 minutes, then remove and let them cool. **5.** While the cookie straws are cooling, make the glaze. **6.** Place the straws with the cookies on a wire rack with a sheet of parchment paper below to catch drips. Spoon the glaze over them, turning them to get glaze on all sides. Let the excess glaze drip off before you transfer the cookies to a sheet of parchment paper. **7.** Let the cookie straws rest until the glaze has stiffened, about 1 hour. Store the cookies in an airtight container. They should be eaten within a couple of days. Without the glaze, they can be kept longer.

WALNUT BROWNIE CAKE WITH WHIPPED CREAM AND BLUEBERRIES

makes one 9-inch (23 cm) round cake

Perfect bluish-purple bells, hanging from flimsy stems... bluebells are lovely, either down by the lake, high up in the mountains, or on top of a cake. Frosted with fluffy whipped cream and topped with refreshing blueberries, this sweet brownie cake gets a summery lift.

Bluebells

bluebell flowers
1 egg white
pinch of salt
superfine white sugar

The bluebells must be prepared at least a couple of hours before they are to be used. You can make them a day in advance to make sure they're dry. Follow the instructions on page 93.

Brownie cake

⅔ cup (150 g) butter
3.5 oz (100 g) bittersweet baking chocolate, coarsely chopped
2 eggs
1 cup (200 g) granulated sugar
⅔ cup (80 g) all-purpose flour
½ tsp vanilla bean seeds, or 1 tsp vanilla sugar
¾ cup (100 g) walnuts, coarsely chopped

Preheat the oven to 325°F (165°C). Line the bottom of a 9-inch (23 cm) round springform pan with parchment paper.

In a saucepan, melt the butter, then remove from the heat. Add the chocolate to the butter and stir until it melts. Let the chocolate mixture cool a little, then transfer it to a mixing bowl.

In a separate bowl, using a handheld mixer, beat the eggs and sugar together until pale in color. Pour the egg mixture into the chocolate, stirring gently. Sift in the flour and add the vanilla seeds, then fold in with a rubber spatula.

In a bowl, toss the walnuts with 2 tsp of flour, then fold them into the batter. (This will keep them from sinking to the bottom.) Pour the batter into the prepared pan and bake for 30 to 35 minutes on the middle rack of the oven. Remove and let the cake cool. Keep it in the refrigerator until ready to serve.

Cream and berry topping

1 cup (250 ml) whipping cream
1 Tbsp granulated sugar
1⅓ cups (200 g) blueberries

Prepare the topping just before serving the cake. In a bowl, using a handheld mixer, whip the cream with the sugar until stiff peaks form. Spread the whipped cream on the cake and top with blueberries. Decorate with the candied bluebells.

Variation: You can use chocolate liqueur cream (page 105) instead of the whipped cream. Other berries or fruit can replace the blueberries.

1. Go for a walk and pick some bluebells. Put them in water until you're ready to use them. **2.** Cut off the flowers, leaving around 1 inch (2.5 cm) of the stem. **3.** Remove the stigma and the pistils inside the bell. **4.** With a fork, whisk the egg white with a pinch of salt. Holding the flowers by the stem, paint the inside of each bluebell with the egg white, then the outside. **5.** Spoon some sugar into the bluebell before you turn it over and sprinkle sugar on the outside. Shake gently so that only a thin layer of sugar remains on both sides. **6.** Attach a small piece of tape to the stem of the flower. Fold the tape over a skewer suspended between two glasses, so the bluebells hang while they dry. You can also place them on parchment paper, with the opening down, but then some of them will lose their lovely shape. The flowers need 2 to 3 hours to dry. You can let them hang overnight. **7.** Cut off the stem where it attaches to the flower. Keep the bluebells in an airtight container if you're not going to use them right away. They can be stored for several months.

LICORICE MACARONS WITH RASPBERRY FILLING

makes 35 macarons

It's so worth it to scramble through the thickets and thorns to pick deep-red raspberries. Each berry contains many little seeds surrounded by juicy pulp—they look like little pearls. These licorice macarons are filled with the taste of summer.

Licorice macarons

¾ cup + 2 Tbsp (85 g) almond flour
¾ cup + 2 Tbsp (110 g) icing sugar
2 tsp licorice root powder
2 medium egg whites (70 g)
3 Tbsp (35 g) granulated sugar
pinch of salt

Sift the almond flour into a bowl. Stir in the icing sugar and licorice root powder, then sift again into another bowl.

In a separate bowl, using a handheld mixer, beat the egg whites at medium speed until foamy. Add the salt. Gradually add the sugar, continuing to beat at medium speed. When all the sugar has dissolved and you have a thick meringue, add the almond flour mixture, beating it into the meringue with a rubber spatula. When the mixture is smooth, fill a piping bag.

Pipe out macarons onto a macaron baking mat or parchment paper, forming circles about 1¼ inches (3.5 cm) in diameter (see page 198 for templates). Tap the baking sheet with the macarons once against the kitchen counter so that any big air bubbles rise to the surface and burst. Let the macarons dry for about 40 minutes on the counter.

Preheat the oven to 250°F (125°C) on the convection setting, or 275°F (135°C) on the regular setting. Bake the macarons for about 15 minutes on the middle rack of the oven (if you're using a regular oven, they may take a few minutes longer). For more detailed instructions, see page 190.

Decoration

½ tsp water
red liquid gel food coloring
¼ cup (50 g) pearl sugar, coarse sugar, or crushed sugar cubes
4 tsp icing sugar
1 tsp licorice root powder
1 tsp water

See page 97 for instructions.

Raspberry filling

1½ cups (200 g) raspberries (fresh or frozen)
¼ cup (50 g) granulated sugar
1 tsp fruit pectin powder

In a saucepan, bring the raspberries and sugar to a boil over medium heat. Reduce the heat and let the mixture simmer for 1 minute before you add the fruit pectin. Continue boiling for 1 minute, then remove from the heat and allow to cool. Transfer to a piping bag and pipe out the filling onto half the macarons, then top with the other halves. Keep them in the refrigerator until ready to serve.

1
2
3
4
5
6

1. To color the pearl sugar, mix a few drops of food coloring with ½ tsp water in a bowl. Stir in the pearl sugar to coat. 2. Spread the sugar onto a baking sheet topped with parchment paper. Bake in the oven at 350°F (175°C) for about 3 minutes. Watch it carefully. It doesn't take long before it starts to melt. 3. When the sugar has melted to the shape of pearls, remove them from the oven and let them cool on the baking sheet. 4. In a bowl, stir together the icing sugar, licorice root powder, and 1 tsp water. Fill a plastic bag with the icing and cut a small hole in the tip. You can also keep the mixture in a bowl and use a toothpick to apply the icing. 5. Use the icing as a glue to attach the sugar pearls. Don't use the bigger pearls; they're too hard. Tweezers make the job of placing the pearls a little easier. 6. Place the pearls on their own or in groups. If you want to place them in the shape of a raspberry, you can use icing to draw the outline.

BLUEBERRY CREPE TORTE

makes one 8.5-inch (22 cm) torte

Have you seen the beautiful colors of blueberry bush leaves at the end of the summer? Grab a bucket for berries and go out foraging! You'll return home with purple blueberry fingers, a bucket of berries, and a few blueberry bush twigs.

Blueberry filling

- 2¾ cups (400 g) blueberries (fresh or frozen)
- ¾ cup (150 g) granulated sugar
- ⅓ cup (75 ml) lemon juice
- 1 Tbsp fruit pectin powder

Combine the blueberries, sugar, and lemon juice in a saucepan over medium heat. Bring to a boil, stirring. Reduce the heat and let it simmer for a few minutes before you stir in the fruit pectin. Let it boil for 1 more minute. Let the filling cool a little before you put it in the refrigerator to cool completely.

Crepes

- 5 eggs
- 4 cups (1 L) 2% milk
- 2¾ cups (350 g) all-purpose flour
- ½ tsp salt
- 2 tsp ground cardamom
- butter (for frying)

Whisk the eggs together with about 1 cup (250 ml) of the milk. In a separate bowl, stir together the flour, salt, and cardamom. Sift the dry ingredients into the egg mixture and whisk until you have a smooth batter. Gradually add the rest of the milk, stirring constantly to avoid lumps. Let the batter sit for about 30 minutes so the flour swells (which makes the crepes lighter).

Heat a little butter in a skillet. Ladle in some batter and swirl it around to coat the bottom of the pan. Cook until the edges are brown and the batter is set, then flip the crepe over and cook for another minute. Repeat with the remaining batter. You will end up with about 12 crepes.

Pile the crepes and cover them with a clean kitchen towel until you're ready to assemble the torte. The crepes should be completely cooled. You can make them a day in advance and keep them in the refrigerator or on the counter, covered with the towel.

Decoration

- 1 cup (150 g) blueberries
- a couple of twigs from a blueberry bush

To assemble the torte, spread a thin layer of blueberry filling on each crepe, and stack the crepes together. Spread a layer on top of the torte, too, so the loose berries will stick. Stick a skewer into the middle of the cake, pull it out, and insert a couple of blueberry bush twigs.

Tip: You can also use ready-made blueberry jam for the filling. Jams of other fruits and berries, or chocolate or nut spreads, also work well. Serve the crepe torte with ice cream, if you like.

SUMMER INTO FALL

The temperature dips, and the air is crisp and fresh. Forests and mountains change color. Robust shades of red, together with brown, orange, and yellow, make the landscape incredibly beautiful. Going for a walk in the pouring rain and then coming home to dry, warm clothes and something freshly baked is the best feeling of all!

VANILLA CLOUDBERRY MACARONS

makes 35 macarons

White cloudberry flowers tie themselves in knots and then turn into juicy berries over the course of the summer. The strong orange color of the cloudberries brightens the bogs where they grow. Enjoy these macarons as you close your eyes and dream yourself back to the mountains.

Vanilla macarons
¾ cup + 2 Tbsp (85 g) almond flour
¾ cup + 2 Tbsp (110 g) icing sugar
¼ tsp vanilla bean seeds, or 1 tsp vanilla sugar
2 medium egg whites (70 g)
pinch of salt
3 Tbsp (35 g) granulated sugar
orange liquid gel food coloring

Sift the almond flour into a bowl. Stir in the icing sugar and vanilla seeds, then sift again into another bowl.

Using a handheld mixer, beat the egg whites in a bowl at medium speed until foamy. Add the salt. Gradually add the sugar, continuing to beat at medium speed. Add the food coloring toward the end, a drop or two at a time. When the sugar has dissolved and you have a thick meringue, add the almond flour mixture, using a rubber spatula to beat it in. When the mixture is smooth, fill a piping bag.

Pipe out macarons onto a macaron baking mat or baking sheet covered in parchment paper, forming circles about 1¼ inches (3.5 cm) in diameter (see page 198). Tap the baking sheet against the kitchen counter to make any large air bubbles rise to the surface and burst. Let the macarons dry for about 40 minutes on the counter.

Preheat the oven to 250°F (125°C) using the convection setting, or 275°F (135°C) on the regular setting. Bake the macarons for about 15 minutes on the middle rack (a few minutes longer in a regular oven). For a more detailed description, see page 190.

Cloudberry filling
2½ cups (300 g) cloudberries
⅓ cup (80 g) granulated sugar
1 tsp fruit pectin powder

Press the cloudberries through a strainer to get rid of the seeds. Make sure you end up with approximately 1½ cups (170 g) of mashed cloudberries. Combine the cloudberries and sugar in a saucepan and bring to a boil over medium heat. Turn down the heat and let it simmer for 5 minutes before you add the fruit pectin. Boil for 1 minute more, then remove from the heat. Let it cool, then fill a piping bag with the mixture.

Decoration
orange liquid gel food coloring
water

In a small bowl, mix a few drops of food coloring with a little water. Use a cotton swab to stamp dots on the macaron shells. The more water you use, the weaker the color will be—you can use different shades if you want.

Pipe out the cloudberry filling onto half of the macaron shells, and place the rest of the shells on top. Keep the macarons in the refrigerator until you're ready to serve them.

Tip: If you can't pick your own berries, you can find cloudberry jam in some stores. You can also use raspberries instead of cloudberries, and red liquid gel food coloring instead of orange for the shells and dots.

NUT CAKE WITH CHOCOLATE LIQUEUR CREAM

makes one 9-inch (23 cm) round cake with 20 mushrooms

When the mushrooms are made of sweet meringue, and the hats are made of chocolate, nobody will complain that they don't like mushrooms! These mushrooms decorate a moist nut cake, frosted with a rich chocolate liqueur cream.

Meringue mushrooms

- 2 medium egg whites (70 g)
- pinch of salt
- ⅔ cup (120 g) granulated sugar
- 1 tsp unsweetened cocoa powder
- 3.5 oz (100 g) bittersweet baking chocolate
- 2 Tbsp icing sugar, more as needed (for assembling mushrooms)

Using a handheld mixer, beat the egg whites at medium speed until foamy. Add the salt. Gradually add the sugar, continuing to beat at medium speed until you have a thick meringue without sugar grains. Fill a piping bag with the meringue. For further instructions, turn to page 107.

In a saucepan, temper the chocolate, following the procedure on page 187 (you can temper the chocolate for the liqueur cream below at the same time, as it's easier to heat up a large portion at once). After you're finished dipping the mushroom hats (see page 107), pour the remaining chocolate onto parchment paper and let it harden again.

Chocolate liqueur cream

- 3.5 oz (100 g) bittersweet baking chocolate
- 1 cup (250 ml) whipping cream
- 2½ Tbsp chocolate liqueur

Chop the re-hardened chocolate from the step above and put it in a mixing bowl. Bring the whipping cream and the chocolate liqueur to a boil and pour over the chocolate. Stir until the chocolate has melted. Let it cool to room temperature, then put the bowl in the refrigerator.

Nut cake

- 1¼ cups (175 g) almonds, chopped
- ⅔ cup (100 g) hazelnuts, chopped
- 3 eggs
- 1 cup (200 g) granulated sugar

Preheat the oven to 325°F (160°C). Line the bottom of a 9-inch (23 cm) round springform pan with parchment paper.

In a bowl, using a handheld mixer, beat the eggs and sugar together at medium speed until pale in color. Fold in the chopped nuts with a rubber spatula. Pour the batter into the prepared pan and bake for 45 minutes on the middle rack of the oven.

Place the pan on a wire rack to cool for 10 minutes, then remove the cake from the springform and transfer it to the rack to cool completely.

Decoration

- chocolate, for grating

When the chocolate liqueur mixture has cooled, beat it to a cream. Spread it over the cooled cake. You may want to grate chocolate over the cake, then place the mushrooms on top. Serve the remaining mushrooms on the side.

Variation: For a child-friendly version, skip the chocolate liqueur. You can also use milk chocolate instead of dark chocolate.

1
2
3
4

1. Preheat the oven to 175°F (75°C) on the convection setting, or 200°F (90°C) on the regular setting. Pipe out 20 mushroom hats and 20 stalks. Sprinkle cocoa powder over the stalks before you put them in the oven. By adding the cocoa powder before, rather than after the drying, you avoid the cocoa powder spreading to the mushroom hats. Dry the meringue in the preheated oven for about 5 hours. 2. When the meringue has cooled, you can cut the tops off the stalks to get a flat area to attach the hats to. 3. Stir the icing sugar with a little water to make a paste. Dip the stalk in the icing and put the hat in place. 4. Dip each hat in the tempered chocolate and place them on parchment paper to dry. Store the mushrooms at room temperature, preferably in an airtight container.

PISTACHIO BROWNIE CAKE WITH TROLL CREAM

makes one 9-inch (23 cm) round pan

Lingonberries, a lowbush cranberry called *tyttebær* in Norwegian, start out as cute white-and-rose-colored bell flowers before they turn into ruby-red berries by the end of the summer. In Norway, they're used to make fluffy, tart troll cream—a pale-pink, airy dessert named for the trolls said to live in the forest where the berries grow. It makes the perfect match for these sweet, dense chocolate brownies.

Brownies

⅔ cup (150 g) butter
3.5 oz (100 g) bittersweet baking chocolate, coarsely chopped
2 eggs
1 cup (200 g) granulated sugar
⅔ cup (80 g) all-purpose flour
⅔ cup (100 g) pistachios

Preheat the oven to 325°F (165°C). Line the bottom of a 9-inch (23 cm) round springform pan with parchment paper.

In a saucepan, melt the butter, then remove from the heat. Stir the chocolate into the hot butter until it melts. Let the mixture cool a bit, then transfer it to a bowl.

In a separate bowl, using a handheld mixer, beat together the eggs and sugar until pale in color. Pour the egg mixture into the chocolate mixture, gently stirring until combined. Sift in the flour, folding it in with a rubber spatula. Stir in the pistachios (you can toss them with 2 tsp flour first so they don't sink to the bottom of the pan).

Pour the batter into the prepared pan and bake for 30 to 35 minutes in the middle of the oven. Remove and let the cake cool. You can refrigerate it until just before serving, when you add the troll cream.

Troll cream

1 cup (80 g) lingonberries
1 tsp water
1 egg white
pinch of salt
5 Tbsp (60 g) granulated sugar

Combine the lingonberries and water in a saucepan over medium heat. Bring to a boil, then remove from the heat.

While the lingonberries are coming to a boil, using a handheld mixer, beat the egg white with the salt at high speed. When stiff peaks have formed, gradually add the sugar, continuing to beat. Add the lingonberries, still beating at high speed until you have a stiff mixture. Fill a piping bag and pipe the cream onto the cake right away (I have used a star tip here). You can also spread the cream with a spoon.

Decorations

icing sugar
lingonberries
pistachios

Sprinkle icing sugar over the cake through a tea strainer. Pipe out the troll cream and decorate with lingonberries and pistachio leaves. You'll find instructions for the leaves on page 112.

Variation: The troll cream can also be served as a dessert on its own: make a larger batch and divide it into serving bowls. You can also use nuts other than pistachios in the brownie cake.

Note: You can find lingonberries at IKEA or at European specialty stores. If you can't find them, fresh cranberries can be substituted.

CINNAMON MACARONS WITH APPLE FILLING

makes 35 macarons

Get out the ladder and a basket! Crisp, juicy apples are finally ready to be harvested. Use them to fill cinnamon macarons and you'll have sweets tasting like apple pie. If you spray them with red, yellow, and green food coloring, you can also mimic the fine color variations of apples.

Cinnamon macarons

- ¾ cup + 2 Tbsp (85 g) almond flour
- ¾ cup + 2 Tbsp (110 g) icing sugar
- 1½ tsp cinnamon
- 2 medium egg whites (70 g)
- pinch of salt
- 3 Tbsp (35 g) granulated sugar

Sift the almond flour into a bowl. Stir in the icing sugar and cinnamon, then sift again into another bowl.

In a separate bowl, using a handheld mixer, beat the egg whites at medium speed until foamy. Add the salt. Gradually add the sugar, continuing to beat at medium speed. When all the sugar has dissolved and you have a thick meringue, add the almond flour mixture, using a rubber spatula to beat it into the meringue. When the meringue is smooth, fill a piping bag. For a more detailed description of how to make macarons, see page 190.

Follow the instructions for assembling the macarons on the next page.

Apple filling

- 2 medium apples, cored and cut in eighths
- 1 Tbsp lemon juice
- ¼ cup (50 g) granulated sugar
- 1 tsp fruit pectin powder

Place the apple pieces in a saucepan with a little water and bring to a boil, then turn down the heat and simmer until the apples are soft. Remove from the heat and drain. Put the apple pieces and lemon juice in a bowl and puree using a handheld blender. Return the pureed apples to the saucepan, along with the sugar, and bring to a boil, stirring constantly. Let boil for a couple of minutes, then add the fruit pectin and boil for 1 more minute. Remove from the heat and let it cool.

Decoration

- 20 pretzel sticks
- yellow, red, and green liquid gel food coloring
- approximately 50 pistachios
- 2 Tbsp icing sugar, more as needed

Follow the instructions for the decoration on the next page.

1. Using a sharp knife, cut the pretzels into pieces ½ inch (1 cm) long. Try to cut as straight as possible. This makes it easier to get them to stand up. 2. Pipe out the macarons onto a macaron baking mat or parchment paper, forming circles 1¼ inches (3.5 cm) in diameter (see page 198 for template). Tap the baking sheet with the macarons once against the kitchen counter so that any large air bubbles rise to the surface and burst. Insert pretzel sticks into half of the macaron shells. Let the macarons dry for about 40 minutes on the counter. Preheat the oven to 250°F (125°C) on the convection setting, or 275°F (135°C) on the regular setting. Bake the macarons for 15 minutes in the middle of the oven (if you're using a regular oven, you may need to bake them for a few minutes longer). 3. Fill three little spray bottles with some water and the liquid gel food coloring. You can find travel spray bottles in many stores. Shake well. The more water, the weaker the color—test until you find the right shade. When the shells have cooled, spray-paint them. You can use more than one color on the same shell. You can also use a toothbrush to spread the dye, but then you'll end up with larger spots. 4. Use a fine grater to file down the pistachios until they look like little leaves. Watch your fingers! You can use a knife to halve them. 5. Mix the icing sugar with a little water to make a paste. Use this as a glue to attach the pistachio "leaves" to the apples. 6. Pipe the apple filling onto the bottoms of the macarons, then put on the top lids. Keep the macarons in the refrigerator until you're ready to serve them.

1
2
3
4
5
6

PISTACHIO MARZIPAN PEARS

makes 20 marzipan pears

When you replace some of the almonds in the marzipan with pistachios, the resulting color will remind you of pears. Then all you need to do is decorate with some pretzels and almonds to make your own extra-sweet pears.

Marzipan pears
1 cup (125 g) unsalted pistachios
1 cup (125 g) almonds
1⅔ cups (200 g) icing sugar
1 egg white

Using a nut grinder, grind the pistachios and almonds into a bowl. Stir in the icing sugar, then grind the mixture one more time. Add the egg white and work everything together with your hands to make a firm dough.

Decoration
2 Tbsp icing sugar, more as needed
10 pretzel sticks
20 almonds

In a small bowl, stir the icing sugar with a little water to make a paste. This will be the glue for the almond "leaves."

Shape pieces of marzipan dough (about 1½ Tbsp each) into small balls. Roll them a little extra on one side so they take the shape of pears.

Stick a piece of pretzel ¾ inch (2 cm) long into the top of the pear. Use an almond to make a little notch near the pretzel. Remove the almond and put a spot of icing there before you return the almond "leaf." Store the marzipan pears in an airtight container.

Variation: These marzipan pears make perfect gifts. You can also make green apples by rolling out small round balls. If you want other colors, you can replace the pistachios in the recipe with additional almonds, and color the dough with liquid gel food coloring.

CHOCOLATE CINNAMON TREE COOKIES

makes 40 cookies

Growth rings can be counted to determine the age of a tree. These cookies definitely will not last as long as their growth rings indicate! Like crispy little brothers of cinnamon buns, they taste so good they'll disappear in the blink of an eye.

Cookies

1 cup (225 g) butter, at room temperature
1 cup (200 g) granulated sugar
1 egg
3 cups (375 g) all-purpose flour
3 tsp ground cardamom
½ tsp salt

Cinnamon filling

⅓ cup (75 g) butter, at room temperature
⅓ cup (75 g) granulated sugar
3 Tbsp cinnamon

Using a handheld mixer, whip the butter and sugar together in a bowl until fluffy. Add the egg and whip some more. Combine the flour, cardamom, and salt in a separate bowl. Add the flour mixture to the egg mixture and work together into a dough using your hands.

In a small bowl, stir together all the cinnamon filling ingredients. It's important the filling is soft so it can be easily spread in a thin layer.

Divide the dough into two parts. Roll one part into a long sausage shape and place it on a sheet of parchment paper. Put another sheet of parchment paper on top so you can roll out the dough without having it stick to the rolling pin. Roll the dough into a thin rectangle, approximately 20 x 8 inches (50 x 20 cm). Remove the top sheet of parchment paper.

Spread a thin layer of half the cinnamon filling on the rectangle, leaving ½ inch (1 cm) along one of the shorter sides. Roll the dough, starting from the side with the filling. Use the bottom sheet of parchment paper to help you roll firmly. Finally, wrap the whole roll in parchment paper. Repeat with the other half of the dough. Put both rolls in the freezer for about 30 minutes. If you leave them for too long, the slices will fall apart when you cut them.

Preheat the oven to 375°F (190°C) and line a baking sheet with parchment paper. Use a sharp knife to cut slices of the cinnamon rolls, between ⅛ and ¼ inch (0.5 cm) thick. Place the slices on the prepared baking sheet and bake for 8 to 10 minutes on the middle rack of the oven. Transfer to a wire rack to cool.

Chocolate edge

7 oz (200 g) bittersweet baking chocolate

Temper the chocolate according to the instructions on page 187. Roll the edges of the cooled cookies in the melted chocolate. Place the cookies on parchment paper and let the chocolate harden at room temperature. Store the cookies in an airtight container.

Tip: If you want your cookies to be completely round, and not flattened on the side the roll lies on, you can follow this instruction before you put the roll in the freezer. Cut open a paper towel tube. Place the roll—with its parchment paper, so it doesn't stick—inside the tube. Tape it shut.

MERINGUE TREES WITH TOASTED ALMONDS

makes 25 meringue trees

Walking along a narrow path with high spruce trees on either side is a magical experience. The sunbeams occasionally make their way through, and the contrast between the sunshine and the shade is remarkable. Make your own fairy-tale forest of sweet meringue trees on a carpet of crunchy almonds.

Meringue trees

3 medium egg whites (100 g)
pinch of salt
¾ cup + 2 Tbsp (180 g) granulated sugar
green liquid gel food coloring

Preheat the oven to 175°F (75°C) on the convection setting, or 200°F (90°C) on the regular setting. Line a baking sheet with parchment paper.

In a bowl, using a handheld mixer, beat the egg whites at medium speed until foamy. Add the salt, which makes the meringue firmer. Gradually add the sugar, continuing to beat at medium speed until you have a thick meringue without grains of sugar. Add a few drops of liquid gel food coloring toward the end. Fill a piping bag with the meringue. I've used a star tip here, but you can also make trees with a round tip.

Pipe out the trees onto the prepared baking sheet, squeezing the bag and pulling upward. Do this a couple of times, piping out several layers on top of each other to make each tree. Place the meringues in the oven to dry for about 5 hours.

Toasted almonds

⅔ cup (120 g) granulated sugar
¼ cup (50 ml) water
2 cups (300 g) almonds
1 Tbsp butter

In a saucepan, bring the sugar and water to a boil over medium heat. Allow to boil for 1 minute, then add the almonds, stirring the whole time. Little by little, the sugar will crystallize. You have to be patient! After 15 to 20 minutes, the sugar will melt again and form an even sheen on the almonds. It's still important to keep stirring. Don't feel tempted to turn up the heat, even if you think the process is slow—if you do, the almonds may burn.

When the almonds are done, stir in the butter. Pour the almonds onto parchment paper right away and immediately separate them with the help of two forks. Allow them to cool, then coarsely chop the desired amount of almonds for the trees and set aside on a plate. Serve the rest whole on the side.

Chocolate

7 oz (200 g) bittersweet baking chocolate

When the meringue trees are done, temper the chocolate. See page 187 for instructions. Dip the bottoms of the trees, first in the chocolate and then in the chopped almonds. Place the trees on parchment paper and let the chocolate harden at room temperature. Store the trees in an airtight container.

Variation: Skip the food coloring if you want white, snow-covered trees. Decorate with silver sugar pearls to make them sparkle, fastening them on with some icing.

RASPBERRY MOUSSE CAKE WITH MINT CHOCOLATE

makes one 9-inch (23 cm) round cake

Spruce needles stay on their trees for many years before they fall off and form a brown carpet on the forest floor. Bring your forest outing home with you and make this fluffy raspberry mousse, with a crust of oatmeal-cookie crumbs and almonds, covered in chocolate needles.

Raspberry mousse cake

5 oz (140 g) oatmeal cookies
⅔ cup (140 g) butter, at room temperature
¾ cup (100 g) almonds, coarsely chopped
3¼ cups (400 g) raspberries, thawed if frozen
4 gelatin sheets
½ cup (110 g) granulated sugar
1⅔ cups (400 ml) whipping cream
¼ tsp vanilla bean seeds, or 1 tsp vanilla sugar or extract

Crush the oatmeal cookies by placing them in a sealed bag and using a rolling pin. It's better to crush them coarsely, not too finely, so the crust will be less dense. In a bowl, stir together the butter, cookie crumbs, and chopped almonds. Press the mixture into the bottom of a 9-inch (23 cm) round springform pan to form an even layer.

Press the raspberries through a strainer to get rid of the seeds. Cover the gelatin sheets in water and let them sit while you combine the mashed raspberries and sugar in a saucepan over low heat. When the sugar has dissolved, remove the saucepan from the heat, squeeze the water out of the gelatin leaves, and dissolve them in the raspberry mixture.

While you wait for the raspberry jelly to cool, whip the cream in a bowl using a handheld mixer. Add the vanilla seeds toward the end. If the raspberry jelly has not yet reached room temperature, put the cream in the refrigerator for the time being.

When the jelly has cooled enough, fold it into the cream with a rubber spatula. Pour the mousse over the cookie crumb crust. Put the cake in the refrigerator for a couple of hours, or overnight. Meanwhile, make the chocolate needles.

Chocolate spruce needles

5 oz (150 g) bittersweet baking chocolate
peppermint oil (optional)

Temper the chocolate according to the instructions on page 187. Add a drop or two of peppermint oil, if you want. Put the chocolate into a piping bag with a small tip. Pipe out long, skinny strips onto parchment paper. Let them harden at room temperature, then break them into pieces ¾ inch (2 cm) long.

Cake sides

about 20 After Eight mint thins

Remove the cake from the springform pan. Place After Eight squares around the edge. The mousse will act as glue. Top the cake with chocolate spruce needles. Keep the cake in the refrigerator until you're ready to serve it.

Note: Gelatin sheets are available online and in gourmet food stores.

MAPLE LEAF COOKIES

makes 25 large and 25 small cookies

Nothing says fall like maple leaves changing color. Red, orange, yellow—it looks like the entire tree is on fire! These crispy cookies taste like Norwegian *krumkaker*—a waffle cookie that's a traditional favorite—and add a genuine fall atmosphere to any setting.

Maple leaves

- 2 Tbsp (30 g) butter, melted and slightly cooled
- 1 egg
- 5 Tbsp (60 g) granulated sugar
- ½ cup (60 g) all-purpose flour, sifted
- red and yellow liquid gel food coloring

Using a handheld mixer, beat the egg and sugar together until pale in color. Fold in the flour with a rubber spatula. Add the melted butter. Let stand for 1 hour. Divide the mixture into 3 bowls and add the food coloring. Make one yellow, one orange, and one red mixture. Further instructions are on page 125.

Variation: You may want to add spices (for instance, cardamom) for a different flavor. The cookies can be eaten on their own, or served with ice cream, carrot cake (page 133), or spice cake (page 131). Add the cookies immediately before you serve the cake, because the moisture in the cake will soften and flatten the cookies. You can use this recipe and technique to make other cookie shapes, too—for instance, butterflies.

1
2
3
4
5

1. To make the stencils, copy the patterns on page 197 (or freehand) on pieces of cardboard or plastic. If you're using plastic, the stencils can be saved and used again. Cut out the leaves. 2. Preheat the oven to 400°F (200°C). Put the stencil on a piece of parchment paper and spread out a thin layer of the cookie mixture. Pick up the stencil and use a spatula to transfer the cookie from the parchment paper to the baking sheet. Make 9 leaves per baking sheet. It's best to stick to one size of stencil per baking sheet to make sure the leaves get evenly baked. 3. Bake the leaves for 3 to 5 minutes in the middle of the oven. Pay close attention—the cookies are done when they begin to brown along the edges. 4. Remove the cookies from the baking sheet and bend them instantly to the desired shape by placing them over spoons or other forms. Use both sides of the spoons so you get leaves with varying shapes. 5. When the cookies have cooled, you can store them in an airtight jar until they're ready to be eaten. Humidity will make them soften and flatten.

CHOCOLATE WOOD WITH BERRIES AND NUTS

makes one chocolate board (7 oz/200 g)

The more weather and wind wood is exposed to, the more its pattern emerges. With the help of a textured wooden board and aluminum foil, you can magically produce edible chocolate wood.

Chocolate wooden board
¼ cup (30 g) pistachios
1 tsp Himalayan salt
¼ cup (30 g) dried sweetened cranberries
7 oz (200 g) chocolate

Coarsely chop the pistachios and combine them in a bowl with the salt and dried cranberries. I've used Himalayan salt here, but you can also use other kinds. Remove the biggest pieces if you're using coarse salt.

Make a mold for the chocolate board, following the instructions on page 129. If you want to make more than one piece, you'll have to make several molds. You can use the same piece of real wood for more than one mold.

Follow the instructions for tempering chocolate on page 187. Use more or less chocolate depending on the size and number of boards you plan to make. You can use any type of chocolate you prefer.

Variation: Only your imagination limits what you can put on the back of the wood. You can use pieces of caramel, potato chips, pink peppercorns, marshmallows, M&M's, or any kinds of nuts, dried fruits, or berries. These chocolate boards make much-appreciated gifts.

1
2
3
4
5
6
7

1. Find an old wooden board with a lot of texture. Maybe you can find driftwood on the shore? Or maybe you have an old wooden fence, worn by weather and wind? In that case, you can bring the aluminum foil outside and make the mold right there. **2.** Place a piece of aluminum foil over the board. **3.** Use your thumb to rub the foil well into the texture of the wood. **4.** Lift the foil and turn the other side up. **5.** Temper the chocolate, following the instructions on page 187. Gently spread the liquid chocolate over your mold, to a thickness of approximately ¼ inch (5 mm). **6.** Immediately sprinkle the pistachio-cranberry mixture on top. **7.** Let the chocolate harden at room temperature before you turn it over and remove the foil. Store the chocolate boards at room temperature.

SPICE CAKE WITH CINNAMON ALMONDS

makes one large baking pan

Acorns can be bitter, but these imitations are sweet. An almond dipped in chocolate and cinnamon takes on the characteristic hat appearance of an acorn. These nuts look good on top of a moist spice cake with a glossy chocolate icing.

Spice cake

- ¾ cup + 2 Tbsp (200 g) butter, melted
- 5½ cups (700 g) all-purpose flour
- 3 cups (600 g) granulated sugar
- 3 tsp cinnamon
- 1 tsp ground cardamom
- 2 tsp ground ginger
- ½ tsp star anise
- ½ tsp salt
- 3 tsp baking soda
- 4 cups (1 L) kefir

Preheat the oven to 350°F (180°C). Line a large baking pan or lasagna pan (around 12" × 16"/30 × 40 cm) with parchment paper.

In a bowl, stir together the flour, sugar, spices, and baking soda. Stir in the kefir and the cooled melted butter. Pour the batter into the prepared pan. Bake for 25 to 35 minutes on the bottom rack of the oven. To determine if the cake is done, stick a toothpick in the middle. If the toothpick comes out clean, the cake is ready.

Place the pan on a wire rack to cool for 10 minutes, then loosen the cake and turn it out on the rack to cool completely.

Cinnamon almonds

- 1 cup (150 g) almonds
- 2 oz (50 g) bittersweet baking chocolate
- 1 tsp cinnamon

While the cake is baking, prepare the almonds. Finely chop the chocolate and slowly melt it in a double boiler or a bowl over a saucepan of water. Put the cinnamon in a small bowl. Dip the wide end of the almond in the chocolate, then in the cinnamon. Let the almonds rest on parchment paper at room temperature until the chocolate has hardened.

Chocolate icing

- 7 oz (200 g) bittersweet baking chocolate
- ⅔ cup (150 ml) whipping cream
- 2 Tbsp (25 g) granulated sugar

Finely chop the chocolate. In a saucepan, heat together the cream and sugar, stirring. When the mixture has almost come to a boil, remove the saucepan from the heat. Add the chocolate and stir with a rubber spatula until you have a smooth, glossy icing. The rubber spatula will prevent you from stirring in too much air. Spread the icing over the cooled cake right away. Decorate with cinnamon almonds and serve the rest on the side.

Variation: You can also make just the cinnamon almonds and wrap them up nicely as a gift.

CARROT CAKE WITH MAPLE TOPPING

makes one 9-inch (23 cm) round cake

A moist cake, full of carrots, walnuts, and raisins. A little cocoa powder on the walnut marzipan carrots makes them look like they've just been pulled out of the dirt.

Carrot cake

⅓ cup (90 g) butter, melted
3 eggs
½ cup (100 g) brown sugar
½ cup (100 g) granulated sugar
1 cup (130 g) all-purpose flour
1 tsp baking powder
1 tsp cinnamon
1 tsp ground cardamom
1 tsp ground ginger
1½ packed cups (200 g) coarsely grated carrots
1 cup (125 g) coarsely chopped walnuts
⅓ cup (50 g) raisins

Preheat the oven to 350°F (175°C). Line the bottom of a 9-inch (23 cm) round springform pan with parchment paper.

In a bowl, using a handheld mixer, beat the eggs and both sugars together until pale in color. Blend in the cooled melted butter.

In a separate bowl, combine the flour, baking powder, cinnamon, cardamom, and ginger. Sift the dry mixture into the egg mixture and stir until you have a smooth batter. Add the grated carrots. You can toss the walnuts and raisins with 1 Tbsp flour before you fold them into the batter with a rubber spatula—this will prevent them from sinking to the bottom.

Pour the batter into the prepared pan and bake the cake for 30 to 40 minutes on the middle rack of the oven. To test if the cake is done, stick a toothpick in the middle—if it comes out clean, the cake is ready.

Remove the cake from the oven and loosen it from the pan. Turn the cake out onto a wire rack covered with parchment paper. Let the cake cool before you cut it horizontally into two layers.

Walnut marzipan carrots

1 cup (125 g) walnuts
1 cup (125 g) almonds
1⅔ cups (200 g) icing sugar
1 egg white
orange liquid gel food coloring
unsweetened cocoa powder (optional)
fresh rosemary leaves (optional)

Grind the walnuts and almonds in a nut grinder. Mix in the icing sugar and grind one more time. Add the egg white and work the mixture together. Add a few drops of orange food coloring until the marzipan is the color of carrots.

Roll out short marzipan carrots. Stand them up and use a knife to cut little transverse stripes. Brush with a little cocoa powder if you want "dirt" on the carrots. Make a small hole at the top of each carrot with a toothpick and insert a few rosemary leaves.

Cream cheese filling and nut topping

¼ cup (65 g) butter, at room temperature
1 cup (125 g) icing sugar
3.5 oz (100 g) plain cream cheese
¾ cup (100 g) coarsely chopped walnuts
⅓ cup (75 ml) maple syrup

In a bowl, using a handheld mixer, whip together the butter, icing sugar, and cream cheese. Spread the cream over the bottom layer of the cake and top with the second layer.

In a separate bowl, stir together the walnuts and maple syrup, then cover the top of the cake with the walnut mixture. Place the carrots on the cake as the picture shows. Serve the rest of the carrots on the side.

FALL INTO WINTER

With the cold comes hoarfrost and ice. Fall colors disappear under a white cover of snow. It's time for Christmas baking, and the kitchen is filled with the smells of spices and nuts.

APPLE PIE WITH CARAMEL AND CHOCOLATE LEAVES

makes 6 small pies

Have you seen how beautiful the fall leaves are after a night of hoarfrost? They sparkle! Make sparkling leaves yourself—chocolate leaves with a sugary edge. Here, they fancy up pecan pies filled with tart applesauce and salted caramel.

Pie shells

½ cup (50 g) pecans, finely chopped
⅓ cup (60 g) brown sugar
¾ cup + 2 Tbsp (110 g) all-purpose flour
¼ tsp salt
⅓ cup (75 g) cold butter

In a bowl, stir together the chopped pecans, brown sugar, flour, and salt. Cut the butter in cubes and use your hands to crumble it together with the dry ingredients. Don't work the dough more than necessary.

Divide the dough into 6 pieces. Press each piece into a 4-inch (10 cm) pie plate, covering the bottom and sides.

Preheat the oven to 325°F (165°C). Put the pie shells in the freezer for 10 minutes before you transfer them to the middle rack of the oven. Bake for 15 minutes. Let cool, then remove the pie shells from the plates.

Applesauce

2 apples, cored and cut in pieces (about 300 g)
1½ Tbsp lemon juice
⅓ cup (75 g) granulated sugar
1½ tsp fruit pectin powder

Put the apple pieces in a saucepan with a little water and bring to a boil, then reduce the heat to simmer. When the apple is soft, pour off the water. Add the lemon juice and puree using a handheld blender. Add the sugar and bring the mixture to a boil, stirring. Let it boil for 2 minutes, then add the fruit pectin and continue to boil for 1 minute. Remove from the heat and let the applesauce cool completely. Fill the pie shells halfway with the applesauce. Put the pies in the refrigerator.

Salted caramel

¾ cup (150 g) granulated sugar
¼ cup (65 g) butter, cubed
⅓ cup (75 ml) whipping cream
¼ tsp salt

In a saucepan, melt the sugar over medium heat, stirring constantly. Don't let the sugar climb up the sides of the saucepan. The sugar will get lumpy before it melts again into a brown syrup. Stir in the butter, then the cream. Cook for 1 minute, stirring constantly so the mixture doesn't burn or boil over. Remove the saucepan from the burner and add the salt.

Let the mixture cool until lukewarm, then pour it over the pies. Store the pies in the refrigerator until ready to serve.

Chocolate leaves

rose leaves
3.5 oz (100 g) bittersweet baking chocolate
1 egg white
granulated sugar
flaked salt

Temper the chocolate according to the instructions on page 187. Follow the instructions on page 139 to make the leaves.

Decorate the pies with chocolate leaves and flaked salt.

Variations: This amount could also make one large pie (9 inches/23 cm). You can use pears instead of apples, or use other nuts in the pie crust.

1. Cut the leaves off unsprayed roses. You can also use leaves from lemon balm or mint. **2.** Place the leaf on a sheet of parchment paper and paint the underside with tempered chocolate. **3.** Immediately move the leaf to another part of the parchment paper to avoid getting chocolate outside the leaf. Repeat with the rest of the leaves. **4.** Let the chocolate harden at room temperature before you remove the leaf. The easiest way to do this is to take hold of the little stem of the leaf and gently pull backward. **5.** Paint the edges of the chocolate leaf with egg white. **6.** Carefully roll the edge in sugar while the egg white is still wet. Repeat with the remaining chocolate leaves. Store them at room temperature in an airtight container. They will keep nicely for several months.

BUN WREATH WITH CRANBERRIES

makes 1 large wreath

Ruby-red Norwegian lowbush cranberries (*tranebær*) are well hidden in the bogs. These tart berries pair well with a sweet bun dough. The berries need a frosty night or two to ripen sufficiently. Roll them in sugar, and they'll look like they're just in from the cold.

Bun wreath

¼ cup (65 g) butter, melted
1 cup (250 ml) whole milk
3 Tbsp (25 g) fresh yeast, or 1½ Tbsp (12 g) active dry yeast
4 cups (500 g) all-purpose flour
⅓ cup (80 g) granulated sugar
1 tsp ground cardamom
½ tsp salt
1 egg yolk

¾ cup (100 g) dried sweetened cranberries
1 small egg white
pearl sugar or other coarse sugar

Combine the melted butter and milk in a mixing bowl. When the mixture is lukewarm, crumble in the yeast. In a separate bowl, stir together the flour, sugar, cardamom, and salt, then add the dry ingredients to the yeast mixture. Add the egg yolk. Knead the dough with your hands for approximately 10 minutes. Cover the bowl with plastic wrap and let the dough rise for about 50 minutes.

When the dough has risen, gently knead it on a floured pastry board. Divide the dough into 2 parts. Divide one of these parts further into 8 smaller pieces. Push a couple of dried cranberries into each piece and roll them into balls, then place them in a wreath formation on a baking sheet, lined with parchment paper. Divide the remaining part of the dough into 20 to 30 smaller pieces. They can vary in size. Push dried cranberries into these pieces before you roll them into small rounds. Place them on and around the wreath. Cover the dough wreath with a clean kitchen towel and let it rise again for about 30 minutes.

Preheat the oven to 425°F (225°C). Brush the wreath with egg white and sprinkle with pearl sugar before you bake it on the middle rack of the oven for 10 minutes. Transfer to a wire rack to cool.

Candied cranberries

2 cups (200 g) fresh cranberries
1 small egg white
granulated sugar

You can find fresh cranberries in the grocery store in fall and winter. Do you want your berries to be covered in frost? Brush them with some egg white and roll them in granulated sugar. For this recipe, I candied about half of the berries.

Decoration

¾ cup (100 g) icing sugar
1 Tbsp water

In a bowl, stir together the icing sugar and water. Drizzle the icing over the wreath. Place the cranberries in the icing to decorate.

Variation: You can use raisins instead of cranberries in the wreath and decorate with grapes. They can be frosted in the same way as the cranberries.

GINGERSNAP MACARONS WITH CREAM CHEESE

makes 35 macarons

When the first snow falls, it begins to feel like Christmas—whether it happens in October or December. The hankering to make snow angels and bake gingersnaps is hard to dismiss. Here, the flavor of gingersnaps is packed into a moist macaron.

Macarons

- ¾ cup + 2 Tbsp (85 g) almond flour
- ¾ cup + 2 Tbsp (110 g) icing sugar
- 1 tsp cinnamon
- 1 tsp ground cloves
- ½ tsp ground ginger
- 2 medium egg whites (70 g)
- pinch of salt
- 3 Tbsp (35 g) granulated sugar

Sift the almond flour into a bowl. Stir in the icing sugar, cinnamon, cloves, and ginger, then sift again into another bowl.

In a separate bowl, using a handheld mixer, beat the egg whites at medium speed until foamy. Add the salt. Gradually add the sugar, continuing to beat at medium speed. When all the sugar has dissolved and you have a thick meringue, add the almond flour mixture, using a rubber spatula to beat it in. When the meringue is smooth, fill a piping bag.

Pipe out macarons onto a macaron baking mat or baking sheet lined in parchment paper, forming circles about 1¼ inches (3.5 cm) in diameter (see page 198 for template). Tap the baking sheet with the macarons once against the kitchen counter so that any big air bubbles rise to the surface and burst. Let the macarons dry on the counter for about 40 minutes.

Preheat the oven to 250°F (125°C) on the convection setting, or 275°F (135°C) on the regular setting. Bake the macarons on the middle rack for 15 minutes (or a few minutes longer if you're using a regular oven). For more detailed macaron instructions, see page 190.

Filling

- 3.5 oz (100 g) plain cream cheese
- 1¼ cups (150 g) icing sugar
- 1 Tbsp lemon juice

In a bowl, blend together the cream cheese, icing sugar, and lemon juice. Fill a piping bag and pipe out the filling onto half of the macaron shells (or you can simply spoon it on). Place the remaining shells on top. Keep the macarons in the refrigerator until serving time.

Decoration

- icing sugar

Sprinkle icing sugar over the macarons through a tea strainer to look like snow.

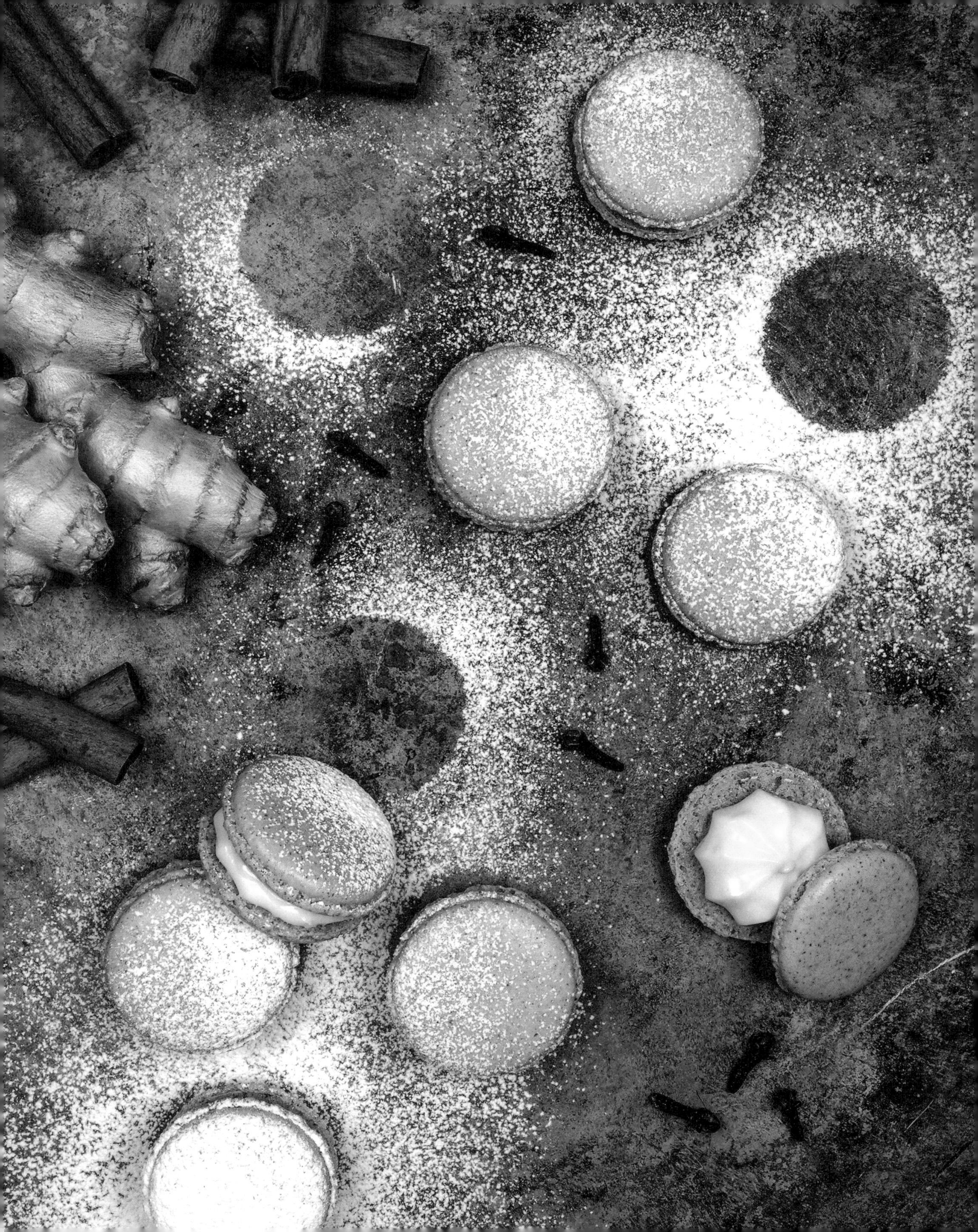

God jul &
godt nytt år!

SNOWFLAKE GINGER COOKIES

makes 27 cookies

It's said that no two snowflakes are alike. They do, however, have one thing in common: the hexagonal structure. A good departure point for drawing a snowflake is to start with three lines crossing each other in the center. Once this base is in place, your imagination can take care of the rest.

Ginger cookies

- ⅓ cup (85 g) butter, at room temperature
- 1 cup (200 g) granulated sugar
- 1 egg
- 6 Tbsp (90 ml) light corn syrup
- 2¼ cups (280 g) all-purpose flour
- 2½ tsp ground ginger
- ½ tsp ground cloves
- 1 tsp baking powder
- ½ tsp salt

In a bowl, using a handheld mixer, whip the butter and sugar together until fluffy. Add the egg and keep whipping, then add the syrup.

In a separate bowl, stir together the dry ingredients. Add them to the butter mixture and knead with your hands until the ingredients are combined. Wrap the dough in plastic wrap and put it in the refrigerator for 30 minutes.

Preheat the oven to 350°F (175°C). Line 3 baking sheets with parchment paper. Roll out balls of approximately 1 Tbsp (25 g) each and flatten them a bit onto the baking sheet. Place 9 cookies on each sheet so they don't run together while baking.

Bake the cookies for 10 to 12 minutes on the middle rack of the oven. Transfer them to a wire rack to cool.

Decoration

- 1 egg white
- 1 tsp lemon juice
- approximately 1⅔ cups (200 g) icing sugar
- granulated sugar

Make icing with the egg white, lemon juice, and icing sugar according to the instructions on page 188. You'll find instructions for making the snowflakes on page 147.

Store the cookies in an airtight container. They make excellent Christmas gifts.

Tip: You can put the cookies in the freezer for 10 minutes before you bake them. This isn't necessary, but it prevents the cookies from spreading.

1. Copy the 6-point pattern on page 198 on a sheet of paper. **2.** Place the cookies over the pattern. **3.** Draw the basic form with the icing. **4.** Then draw the rest of the snowflake—symmetrically, if possible. If you need ideas, you can find them on page 197. **5.** Sprinkle granulated sugar over the snowflake while the icing is still wet. Then it will sparkle like a real snowflake. **6.** Gently tap off any excess sugar.

HAZELNUT COOKIES WITH STAR ANISE

makes 35 cookies

While most things in nature turn brown through the fall, spruce trees stay green all year round. These hazelnut cookies are made special with star anise, which adds a slight taste of licorice. Decorate the cookies with needles that look like a Christmas tree.

Cookies

- 1 cup (225 g) butter, at room temperature
- 1 cup (200 g) granulated sugar
- 1 egg
- 2½ cups (300 g) all-purpose flour
- 2 tsp ground star anise
- 1 tsp salt
- 1 tsp baking powder
- 1 cup (150 g) hazelnuts, finely chopped
- 7 oz (20 g) pretzel sticks

Using a handheld mixer, whip the butter and sugar together until fluffy. Add the egg and keep whipping.

In a separate bowl, stir together the flour, anise, salt, and baking powder. Stir in the hazelnuts, then add the dry ingredients to the butter mixture. Knead the dough and form into a ball. Cover the bowl and let it rest in the refrigerator for 30 minutes.

Preheat the oven to 375°F (190°C). Line a baking sheet with parchment paper. Divide the dough into pieces of around 1 Tbsp (25 g) each and flatten each cookie into oval shapes on the baking sheet, using your fingers or a rolling pin. They should be ⅛ to ¼ inch (3 to 5 mm) thick. Press pieces of pretzels into the cookies in branch shapes.

Bake for 8 to 10 minutes on the middle rack of the oven. Transfer the cookies to a wire rack to cool.

Spruce needles

- 1 egg white
- 1 tsp lemon juice
- 1⅔ cups (200 g) icing sugar
- green liquid gel food coloring

Follow the instructions to make the icing on page 188, using the egg white, lemon juice, and icing sugar, and coloring the icing green. Transfer to a piping bag with a small tip.

Pipe thin, straight lines onto the cookies, going outward from the pretzels so they look like needles on a tree. You can draw them in layers and in different directions. If you want snow on the twigs, sprinkle some icing sugar over the cookies through a tea strainer before serving. Store them in an airtight container.

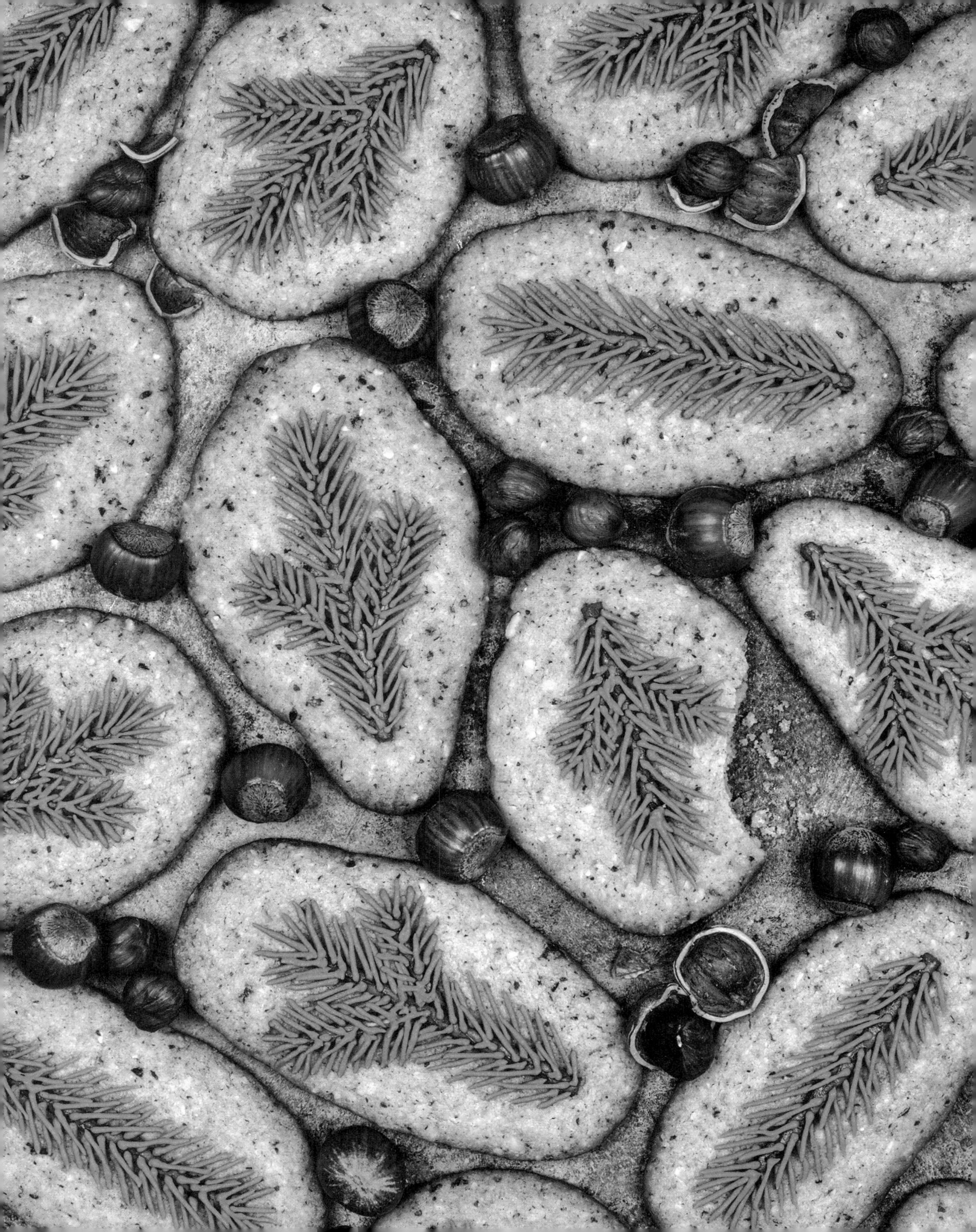

GOD JUL
& GODT NYTT ÅR

GINGERSNAP PINECONES WITH COCOA

makes 70 ginger cookies

Just making this cookie dough conjures up a Christmassy feeling. The house is filled with the aromas of cinnamon, ginger, and cloves. It's almost impossible not to hum a Christmas carol while they're in the oven. These pinecones require neither a rolling pin nor a cookie cutter.

Ginger cookies
½ cup (125 g) butter
½ cup (100 g) granulated sugar
½ cup (125 ml) light corn syrup
⅓ cup + 2 Tbsp (100 ml) whole milk
2½ cups (300 g) all-purpose flour
½ tsp pepper
1½ tsp ground ginger
1 tsp cinnamon
½ tsp ground cloves
1 tsp baking powder
½ tsp salt

Cut the butter into cubes and put them in a mixing bowl. In a saucepan, combine the sugar, syrup, and milk and bring to a boil, stirring. Watch the saucepan carefully so the milk doesn't boil over. Remove from the heat and pour the hot mixture over the butter. While you let the mixture cool, combine the rest of the ingredients in a separate bowl.

When the butter mixture is lukewarm, add the dry ingredients to the butter mixture and stir. Form the dough into a ball and cover in plastic wrap, then place it in the refrigerator for a couple of hours, or overnight. It's easier to work this dough when it's chilled, so leave the remaining dough in the refrigerator while you work on the pinecones.

Decoration
unsweetened cocoa powder

Preheat the oven to 350°F (175°C) and line a baking sheet with parchment paper. Follow the instructions on page 153 to shape the pinecones.

Place the cookies on the baking sheet and bake for about 10 minutes on the middle rack of the oven, then remove and allow to cool. Store the pinecone cookies in an airtight container or wrap them up as a Christmas gift.

Tip: The dough can also be rolled with a rolling pin and cut with cookie cutters.

1. Take approximately 2 tsp (10 g) of the dough at a time and roll out oblong sausage shapes, narrower at one end. **2.** Put the shapes on a sheet of parchment paper, with the narrow ends toward you. Flatten the cookies with your fingers to a thickness of about ⅛ inch (3 mm). **3.** Take out a sharp knife. Hold the knife flat so you can use the tip to make a triangular impression in the dough. Start at the top of the pinecone. Make 3 triangles next to each other. **4.** On the next line, press the knife down between the triangles of the first line. **5.** Repeat this all the way down the pinecone. Repeat with the remaining pinecones. **6.** Bake the cookies as instructed on page 151 and let them cool. **7.** Dip a small brush in cocoa powder and brush each cookie from the bottom to the top. The cocoa gathers in the knife grooves and the pinecone pattern will emerge.

NORWEGIAN ALMOND CAKE WITH COCONUT FROSTING

makes 8 almond cake rings

It's early on Christmas Eve morning in Norway. Outdoors it's dark and cold; indoors the lights on the Christmas tree are glowing. The fragrance of the tree fills the entire room, and the atmosphere is magical. This recipe makes a delicious Norwegian-style almond cake with the flavor of coconut. The perfect thing for the Christmas dessert table!

Star
1⅔ cups (200 g) icing sugar
1 egg white
1 tsp lemon juice

If you want an icing star at the top of the almond cake tree, make it first, preferably a day ahead so it has time to dry completely. I've used a snowflake from page 162 as a star. You'll find the instructions for the icing on page 188.

Almond cake (*Kransekake*)
1¾ cups (250 g) almonds
1⅔ cups (200 g) icing sugar
1 Tbsp all-purpose flour
1 egg white
1 Tbsp lemon juice

Grind the almonds in a nut grinder. In a bowl, stir together the ground almonds, icing sugar, and flour. Add the egg white and lemon juice, and work the dough well with your hands. Roll out sausage shapes the thickness of fingers, then form them into 8 rings using the templates on page 200. Roll a small ball of dough, then flatten it a bit. It will be the top of the tree. Lay the rings and ball on baking sheets lined in parchment paper, and put them in the freezer for 10 minutes before baking.

Preheat the oven to 350°F (180°C). Bake the rings on the middle rack of the oven for about 10 minutes. Transfer to a wire rack to cool.

Coconut frosting
2 Tbsp water, divided
green liquid gel food coloring
1 cup (100 g) unsweetened shredded coconut
1¼ cups (150 g) icing sugar
1 Tbsp lemon juice

Preheat the oven to 350°F (180°C). In a medium bowl, mix 1 Tbsp of the water with a few drops of food coloring. Add the shredded coconut and stir to coat. Spread the coconut on a baking sheet lined with parchment paper and place it in the oven to dry for a couple of minutes.

Meanwhile, combine the icing sugar, lemon juice, and remaining water in a bowl. Spread the icing on the almond rings and ball, icing the top but not the underside. Cover with the green shredded coconut. Set aside a little icing for attaching the silver balls. Let the coconut dry for an hour before you assemble the cake.

Decoration
silver sugar pearls

Place the rings loosely on top of each other, from largest to smallest. Finish with the flattened ball. Apply silver sugar pearls with the help of the icing. You may want to put two sewing pins on either side of the star to support it while the icing dries—but remember to remove the pins before you serve the cake! To serve, remove one ring of the cake at a time.

CHOCOLATE SPOONS WITH CINNAMON AND STAR ANISE

makes 10 tablespoons

Find a dark place one starlit evening and look up. The darker it is around you, the more stars you'll see in the sky. There's no limit! Snuggle on your couch with a throw and a cup of hot chocolate when you return to the warmth again.

Chocolate
- 7 oz (200 g) bittersweet baking chocolate
- 2 tsp cinnamon
- ½ tsp ground star anise

Temper the chocolate according to the instructions on page 187. If you're going to serve the spoons right away, you don't have to temper the chocolate—you can just gently heat it in a double boiler or a bowl over a saucepan of hot water. Stir in the cinnamon and anise. Put the mixture in a piping bag and pipe the chocolate onto 10 tablespoons.

Decoration
- 10 whole star anise
- edible gold spray (optional)

Place a whole star anise on each spoon before the chocolate hardens. If you want the stars to shine, you can spray them with edible gold spray before you place them on the chocolate. Keep the spoons at room temperature.

Serving
- ⅔ cup (150 ml) milk per spoon

Heat the milk to a comfortable drinking temperature and serve it in a cup. Stir with the chocolate spoon.

Tip: These chocolate spoons make great Christmas gifts. You can find pretty spoons at flea markets or in second-hand stores. You can also use disposable wooden spoons.

A NEW YEAR

There is magic in the blue light during the cooler half of the year. The low sun creates fantastic shadows and snow that sparkles.

CHOCOLATE PEANUT CUPCAKES

makes 12 cupcakes

Let snowflakes land on your mitten. Study them carefully. They're so beautiful! It's incredible that something so small can be so intricate; each snowflake is a tiny, unique piece of art. Now you can make your own pieces of art in the form of brownie cupcakes topped with snowflakes made of icing.

Snowflakes

- 1 egg white
- 1 tsp lemon juice
- approximately 1⅔ cups (200 g) icing sugar

Make the snowflakes the day before you're going to use them, as they need time to dry. Follow the instructions on page 188 for making the icing. Transfer the prepared icing to a piping bag and cut a small hole, or use a tip with a small opening. Follow the instructions on the next page for making the snowflakes.

Cupcakes

- ⅔ cup (150 g) butter
- 3.5 oz (100 g) bittersweet baking chocolate
- 2 eggs
- 1 cup (200 g) granulated sugar
- ¾ cup + 1 Tbsp (100 g) all-purpose flour
- ⅔ cup (100 g) salted peanuts

Preheat the oven to 400°F (200°C). Line a 12-cup muffin pan with cupcake liners.

Melt the butter in a saucepan, then remove it from the heat. Coarsely chop the chocolate and add it to the melted butter, stirring until it melts. Leave the chocolate mixture to cool.

In a mixing bowl, briefly whisk together the eggs and the sugar. Stir in the chocolate mixture, then sift in the flour and fold it in with a rubber spatula. Finally, fold in the peanuts.

Fill the cupcake liners with batter. Bake the cupcakes for about 15 minutes on the middle rack of the oven, then remove and let them cool.

Decoration

- icing sugar

When the cupcakes have cooled, stick an icing snowflake into the middle of each one. Sift some icing sugar over the cupcakes.

Variation: You can use other nuts instead of peanuts. You can also add chopped dried fruit to the batter.

1. Place a piece of paper over the snowflakes on page 199. Trace the ones you want to use. You can, of course, also draw snowflakes freehand. **2.** Lay a piece of parchment paper over your drawings. You can fasten the paper to the table with tape so it stays in place. **3.** Use the icing to draw the snowflakes on the parchment paper. **4.** Let the snowflakes dry completely overnight before you gently remove them from the parchment paper with a flat spatula. It's not the end of the world if some of the snowflakes lose an arm or two. If you stick that end into the cupcake, no one will ever know!

1
2
3
4

MACARONS WITH VANILLA BUTTERCREAM

makes 35 macarons

Sunbeams bouncing off ice crystals make the snow sparkle. It looks as if someone has knocked over a big jar of glitter on the winter landscape. Spectacular! A little sugar will make these macarons sparkle, too.

Macarons

¾ cup + 2 Tbsp (85 g) almond flour
¾ cup + 2 Tbsp (110 g) icing sugar
2 egg whites
pinch of salt
3 Tbsp (35 g) granulated sugar
blue liquid gel food coloring

Sift the almond flour into a bowl. Stir in the icing sugar, then sift the mixture again into another bowl.

Using a handheld mixer on medium speed, beat the egg whites until foamy. Add the salt. Gradually add the granulated sugar, continuing to beat the mixture at medium speed. Once all the sugar has dissolved and you have a thick meringue, fold in the food coloring with a rubber spatula, adding a drop at a time until it's the color you want. Add the almond flour mixture and use the spatula to beat it into the meringue. When the mixture is smooth, transfer it to a piping bag.

Line a baking sheet with parchment paper, or use a macaron baking mat. Pipe out the macarons onto the baking mat or parchment paper, forming circles about 1¼ inches (3.5 cm) in diameter (see page 198). Tap the baking sheet with the macarons once against the kitchen counter so that any big air bubbles rise to the surface and burst. Let the macarons dry on the counter for about 40 minutes, until no longer sticky to the touch.

Meanwhile, preheat the oven to 250°F (125°C) on the convection setting, or 275°F (135°C) on the regular setting. Bake the macarons for 15 minutes on the middle rack of the oven, or a few minutes longer if you're using the regular oven setting. Remove and allow to cool.

For more detailed instructions on making macarons, see page 190.

Decoration

granulated sugar
water

Sprinkle some sugar onto a plate. Brush the top of each macaron shell with water, then dip it in the sugar.

Vanilla buttercream

⅓ cup (75 g) butter, at room temperature
1⅔ cups (200 g) icing sugar
1 Tbsp milk
¼ tsp vanilla bean seeds, or 1 tsp vanilla sugar or extract

Using a handheld mixer, whip the butter and icing sugar together until fluffy. Add the milk and whip some more. Stir in the vanilla seeds.

Transfer the buttercream to a piping bag (I have used a star tip here). Top one macaron with the buttercream, then sandwich with another macaron. Repeat with the remaining macarons. (You can also spoon the buttercream onto the macarons.)

Keep the macarons in the refrigerator until you're ready to serve them.

NUTTY COCONUT CAKE WITH STRAWBERRY CREAM

makes one 9-inch (23 cm) round cake

There's magic in the forest when the spruce trees are covered with snow. White as far as you can see! This cake has a crackly crust and a moist, nutty filling. Topped with whipped cream and ice-cream cones covered in shredded coconut, it's a true winter cake.

Winter spruce trees

ice-cream cones
pearl sugar or other coarse sugar
unsweetened shredded coconut
1 egg white
around 1½ cups (180 g) icing sugar

Combine the coarse sugar and shredded coconut on a plate. To make the icing, in a bowl, beat the egg white and add the icing sugar until it reaches the right consistency. Make as many trees as you want, following the instructions on page 168.

Nut cake

3 eggs
1 cup (200 g) granulated sugar
1 cup (150 g) almonds, chopped
¾ cup (100 g) walnuts, chopped
⅓ cup (30 g) unsweetened shredded coconut

Preheat the oven to 325°F (160°C). Line the bottom of a 9-inch (23 cm) round springform pan with parchment paper.

Using a handheld mixer, beat the eggs and the sugar at medium speed until pale in color. Fold in the almonds, walnuts, and shredded coconut with a spatula. Pour the batter into the prepared pan and bake the cake for about 45 minutes on the middle rack of the oven. Remove from the oven and place the pan on a wire rack to cool for 10 minutes, then loosen the cake and transfer it to the rack to cool completely.

Strawberry-chocolate cream

1 cup (150 g) strawberries
3.5 oz (100 g) chocolate (use your favorite kind)
1¼ cups (300 ml) whipping cream
2 Tbsp (25 g) granulated sugar
3 Tbsp (20 g) unsweetened shredded coconut

Chop the strawberries and chocolate into small pieces. Using a handheld mixer, whip the cream with the sugar in a bowl until fluffy. Transfer half of the whipped cream to another bowl and fold in the chocolate and strawberries. Leave the rest of the whipped cream as is.

To assemble, first spread the strawberry-chocolate cream on the cake, then top with the plain whipped cream. Place the cone trees on the cake and sprinkle the shredded coconut all over.

Variation: Color the icing and shredded coconut green (see page 33) and replace the strawberry cream with the chocolate liqueur cream from page 105. Then you'll have a forest cake for the snow-free months.

Note: You can find pearl sugar in European specialty stores. If you don't have it, you can use any kind of coarse sugar or crushed sugar cubes.

1. With a serrated knife, gently saw the bottoms off the ice cream cones so they stand up straight. Make trees of different heights. **2.** Spread icing on the outside of each cone. To make this easier, hold the cone by placing two fingers inside and opening them gently toward the cone walls. **3.** Roll each cone in the shredded coconut mixture. **4.** Let the cone trees dry for an hour before placing on the cake. If you must use them right away, handle them very gently.

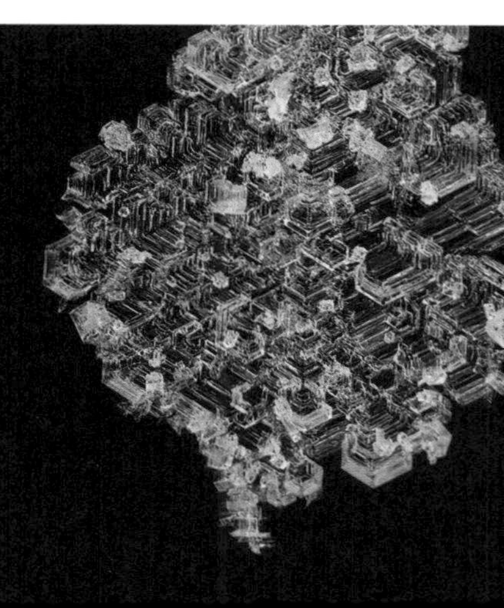

CHOCOLATE COFFEE MOUSSE

makes 8 glasses

Extra-cold days bring with them incredible hoarfrost, intricate crystalline structures worth freezing your toes off to enjoy. The crystallized sugar formations jutting from this decadent mousse are easy to make, and equally deserving of a closer look.

Sugar shards

3 cups (625 g) granulated sugar
1 cup (250 ml) water

Make the sugar shards 2 days before you are ready to use them so the crystals have time to grow. In a saucepan, bring the sugar and water to a boil. When the sugar has dissolved, transfer the syrup to a heatproof dish (approximately 8" × 11"/20 × 30 cm). Leave it at room temperature for about 2 days.

Crack the surface with a knife and gently lift out the shards. Rinse them under running water and gently shake off the excess before you lay them to dry on parchment paper, with the points of the crystals facing down. Once dry, the shards can be stored in a jar for several months.

Frosty edge

1 egg white, lightly beaten
granulated sugar

Place a thin layer of egg white on one plate and a layer of sugar on another. Dip the rim of each serving glass first in the egg white, then in the sugar. Let stand to dry. You can use water instead, but the egg white gives a smoother edge.

Mousse

5 oz (150 g) bittersweet baking chocolate, coarsely chopped
3 eggs, separated
pinch of salt
3 Tbsp (45 ml) strong coffee, cooled
⅓ cup + 1 Tbsp (50 g) icing sugar
1¼ cups (300 ml) whipping cream

Melt the chocolate in a double boiler over low heat. Remove from the heat and let it cool slightly.

Using a handheld mixer, beat the egg whites with the salt until stiff peaks form. In a separate bowl, whisk the egg yolks together with the melted chocolate, coffee, and icing sugar. Fold the egg whites into this mixture using a rubber spatula.

In another bowl, whip the cream using a handheld mixer, then fold it into the chocolate mixture. Transfer the mousse into the prepared glasses and refrigerate for at least an hour, or longer if possible.

Decoration

2.5 oz (75 g) white chocolate

Grate some white chocolate over the mousse and stick a sugar shard into each glass. Leave the mousse in the refrigerator until you are ready to serve it.

Variation: Make the chocolate mousse more child-friendly by skipping the coffee and using milk chocolate.

LEMON ICE CREAM CAKE WITH MARZIPAN SNOWBALLS

makes one 9-inch (23 cm) round cake

Sometimes, when new snow is falling, nature makes its own snowballs: a few snowflakes start rolling together, then grow bigger and bigger. So much fun! You can make your own snowballs out of marzipan and roll them in sugar to add sparkle—a perfect decoration for this refreshing ice cream cake with a cookie crumb crust.

Cookie crumb crust

5 oz (140 g) oatmeal cookies
⅓ cup (85 g) butter, at room temperature

Crush the cookies coarsely by placing them in a sealed bag and using a rolling pin. You don't want the crumbs to be too fine, because the crust will then be denser.

In a bowl, stir together the crumbs and the butter. Press the mixture into a 9-inch (23 cm) round springform pan to form an even layer on the bottom.

Lemon ice cream

3 egg yolks
¾ cup (140 g) granulated sugar
zest of 1 lemon
⅓ cup (75 ml) lemon juice
1¼ cups (300 ml) whipping cream
¼ tsp vanilla bean seeds, or 1 tsp vanilla sugar or extract

Using a handheld mixer, beat the egg yolks and sugar together until pale yellow. Gently stir in the lemon zest and juice.

In a separate bowl, whip the cream until fluffy, adding the vanilla seeds at the end. Gently fold the egg mixture into the whipped cream. Pour the batter over the cookie crumb crust and cover the pan with plastic wrap or aluminum foil. Place the cake in the freezer overnight.

Marzipan snowballs

1¾ cups (250 g) raw almonds
1⅔ cups (200 g) icing sugar
1 egg white
granulated sugar, for rolling

Blanch the almonds by pouring boiling water over them and letting them sit for one minute. Drain the almonds in a strainer and rinse with cool water, then pat dry with a paper towel and remove the skins with your fingers. Place them on a clean kitchen towel to dry. When the almonds are dry, grind them using a nut grinder. Combine the ground nuts with the icing sugar in a bowl and put the mixture through the grinder one more time. Add the egg white and work the dough with your hands until combined.

Place some granulated sugar on a plate. Make marzipan marbles of varying sizes and roll them in the sugar. Store the snowballs in an airtight container until you're ready to use them.

Remove the cake from the freezer 10 minutes before serving. Place some marzipan snowballs on the cake and serve the rest on the side.

Variation: You can add some lemon zest to the marzipan for a more refreshing flavor.

ORANGE CAKE WITH WHITE CHOCOLATE MOUNTAINS

makes one large baking pan

Beaming sun, a blue sky, and snow-covered peaks. Time to put on your skis for an early-spring run in the mountains. Maybe it's warm enough for you to roll up your sleeves? Later, enjoy an after-ski coffee break in a sunny spot with this moist orange cake, accented with white chocolate.

Chocolate mountains

7 oz (200 g) white chocolate
approximately ¾ cup (150 g) granulated sugar

Follow the instructions on page 177 to make the mountains.

Orange cake

⅔ cup (150 g) butter
4.5 oz (130 g) white chocolate
4 eggs
1¼ cups (250 g) granulated sugar
¾ cup + 2 Tbsp (200 ml) buttermilk
zest of 2 oranges
½ cup (125 ml) orange juice
2¼ cups (270 g) all-purpose flour
4 tsp baking powder

Preheat the oven to 350°F (180°C) and line a large baking pan or lasagna pan (around 12" × 16"/30 × 40 cm) with parchment paper.

Melt the butter in a saucepan, then remove it from the heat. Coarsely chop the chocolate and stir it into the hot butter until it melts. While the mixture is cooling, in a bowl, beat the eggs and sugar together using a handheld mixer. Gently stir in the chocolate mixture, buttermilk, orange zest, and juice.

In another bowl, stir together the flour and baking powder. Sift the flour mixture into the batter and fold it in with a rubber spatula. Pour the batter into the baking pan and bake the cake on the middle rack for about 15 minutes. To determine if the cake is done, stick a toothpick in the middle. If the toothpick comes out clean, the cake is ready.

Place the pan on a wire rack to cool for 10 minutes, then loosen the cake and turn it out on the rack to cool completely.

Buttercream

1 cup (225 g) butter, at room temperature
4 cups (500 g) icing sugar
3 Tbsp buttermilk

Using a handheld mixer, whip the butter and icing sugar together until fluffy. Mix in the buttermilk. Transfer the buttercream to a piping bag. Cut a large hole in the bag and pipe out small piles on the cake. (You can also spread the buttercream unevenly over the cake to add variety to the landscape.)

Place the white chocolate mountains in the cream. Finally, sift some icing sugar over everything to make more snow.

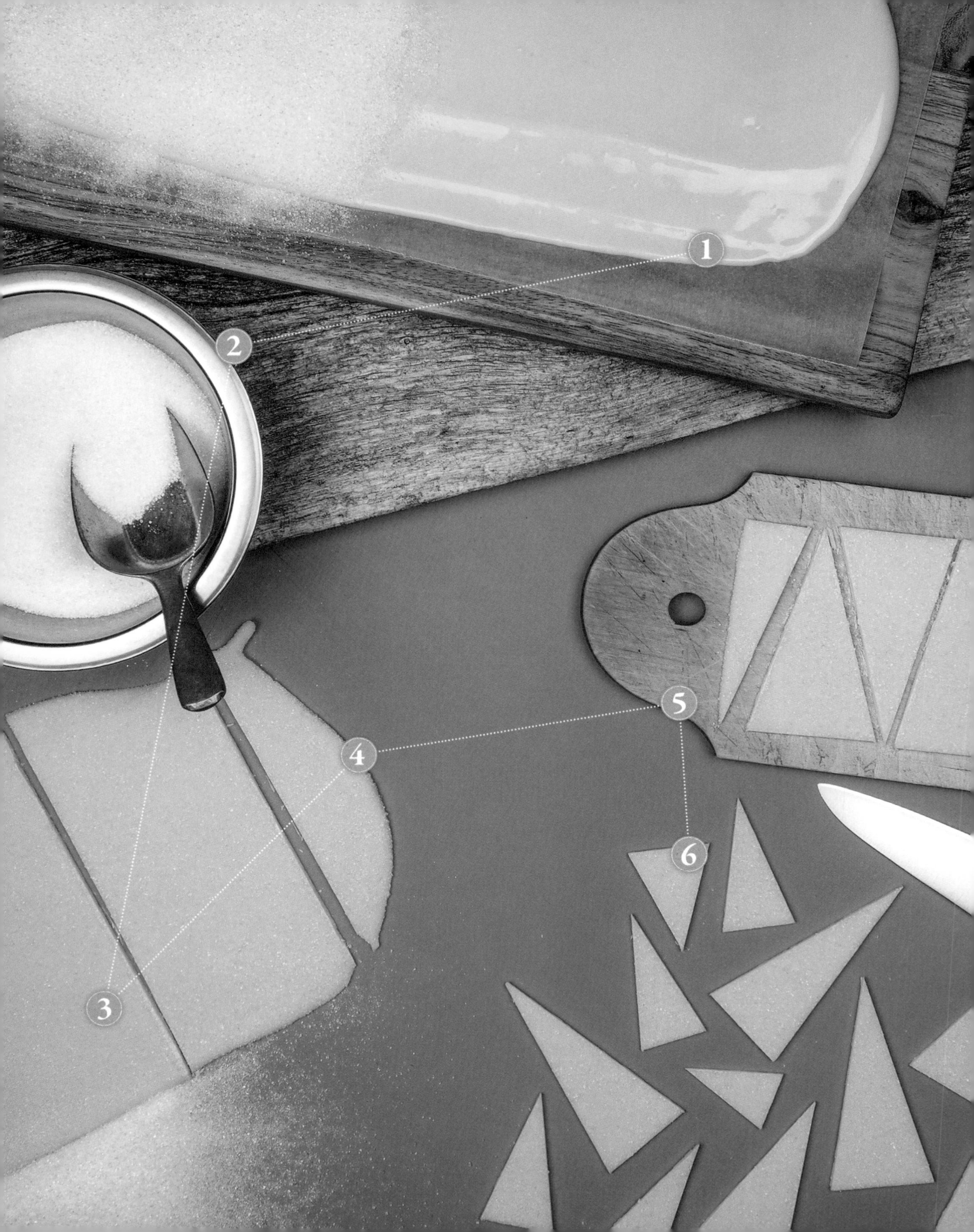
1
2
3
4
5
6

1. Temper the chocolate according to the instructions on page 187. Spread the tempered chocolate on a sheet of parchment paper. 2. While the chocolate is still soft, sprinkle a generous layer of sugar on top. Let it harden at room temperature. 3. When the chocolate has hardened, loosen it from the parchment paper and remove the excess sugar. 4. With a sharp knife, cut the chocolate into strips. The wider the strip, the taller the mountain. 5. Cut the strips on the diagonal to make the mountains. 6. Store the mountains at room temperature until you're ready to use them.

CHEESECAKE WITH CINNAMON-CHOCOLATE CRUST

makes one 9-inch (23 cm) round cake

Remember making paper snowflakes as a child? It was always so exciting to unfold the sheet of paper and see how your snowflake turned out. Get some paper and a pair of scissors, and with a little more effort you can make this delicious cheesecake with its impressive snowflake pattern.

Cinnamon-chocolate crust
9 oz (250 g) oatmeal cookies
4 tsp cinnamon
¾ cup (160 g) butter, at room temperature
2 oz (50 g) bittersweet baking chocolate

Put the cookies in a sealed bag and crush them coarsely using a rolling pin. You don't want the crumbs to be too fine. Transfer the cookie crumbs to a bowl and stir in the cinnamon, then add the butter. Coarsely chop the chocolate and stir it in. Press the cookie crumb mixture into a 9-inch (23 cm) round springform pan to form an even layer on the bottom.

Cheesecake
1 cup (250 ml) orange juice
2 Tbsp granulated sugar
5 gelatin sheets
7 oz (200 g) plain cream cheese
1 cup (120 g) icing sugar
1 tsp vanilla sugar or extract
1⅓ cups (300 g) light sour cream
1¼ cups (300 ml) whipping cream

Strain the orange juice into a small saucepan, add the sugar, and bring to a boil. Meanwhile, put the gelatin in a bowl of cold water for 5 minutes. When the juice boils, remove the saucepan from the heat, then squeeze the water out of the gelatin sheets and add them to the hot orange juice to dissolve. Allow to cool at room temperature.

In a bowl, blend together the cream cheese, icing sugar, and vanilla sugar. Stir in the sour cream. In another bowl, whip the cream until fluffy using a handheld mixer.

When the orange jelly has reached room temperature, gently fold it into the cream cheese mixture with a spatula. Finally, fold in the whipped cream. Pour the mixture over the prepared crust and put it in the refrigerator. Let it chill for a couple of hours, or overnight.

Decoration
unsweetened cocoa powder
sliced oranges

While the cake is in the refrigerator, make the paper snowflakes, following the instructions on page 181.

Loosen the cake from the pan. Place the paper snowflakes on the cake and sift the cocoa powder on top. Then, gently lift off the paper snowflakes. Keep the cake in the refrigerator until you are ready to serve it, with the sliced oranges on the side.

Variation: Gelatin sheets are available online and in gourmet food stores. You can also use jelly powder instead of the orange juice and gelatin. Follow the package instructions, but limit the amount of water to 1 cup (250 ml).

Template to measure 30°.

1. Cut a square of paper, approximately 4 inches (10 cm) on each side. **2.** Fold the square into a triangle. **3.** Fold the sheet again. Now you will have a right triangle, where one of the angles is 90°. **4.** To give the snowflake six sides, which all snowflakes have, you have to fold the paper in three. Start by drawing a helping line 30° from the bottom of the triangle. Use a protractor or the template on the opposite page. The upper part will then be 60°. **5.** Fold the 60° angle in two toward you. **6.** Fold along the helping line, but backward, in the opposite direction. **7.** Draw any pattern you want. You'll find some ideas on the opposite page, but you can also draw freehand. **8.** Cut out the pattern. **9.** To flatten the snowflakes, which will give you the best result when you sprinkle cocoa powder over them, you can iron them (without steam). **10.** Fold small pieces of tape and attach them to the top side of the paper snowflakes. Lift the papers with the help of the tape. **11.** Place the paper snowflakes on the cake and sprinkle cocoa powder over them through a tea strainer. Gently remove the paper. Don't leave the paper on the cake too long—it will get stuck.

BAKING TIPS

Many of my tips and tricks are spread throughout the book, but here are some more general tips. The most important pieces of advice I want to give you are have fun while you bake, dare to try new things, and test any ideas you have.

Recipes	Read through the whole recipe before you begin. Then there are no surprises along the way. Maybe you want to change something? Make notes beside the recipe for future reference. Tastes differ. Do you want your baking to be sweeter? More tart? Saltier?
Measurements and Weights	Measure all the ingredients before you start baking. Then the boring part is out of the way, and the fun can begin. I prefer to use weight rather than volume. Weight is more precise—1 cup of flour can vary a lot. I also prefer using measuring spoons to spoons from the cutlery drawer, for the same reason. I've provided volume measurements alongside the weight ones, but it's worth investing in a small kitchen scale to make your baking more exact.
Ingredients	Having all your ingredients at the same temperature will often lead to better baking results. I always put eggs out on the kitchen counter a little while before I start baking. Room-temperature eggs are especially important in meringue-based desserts.
Baking	All ovens are different. You may have to adjust both the temperature and the baking time. Does your oven bake best toward the back? Then turn whatever you are baking halfway through the baking time.
Egg Whites	When egg whites are to be beaten until they form stiff peaks, the bowl and your tools have to be free from grease.

52 °C
45 °C
45 °C
28 °C
27 °C
26 °C
31 °C
30 °C
29 °C
1
2
3
4
5
6
7

CHOCOLATE TEMPERING

For your chocolate not to melt at the first touch, and also to stay glossy and hard, you have to temper it. Professionals often use a method called *tabling* the chocolate. The method I describe here is easier to accomplish in a small kitchen. It's well worth your time to spend a few minutes learning how to temper chocolate. It will be useful. And it will make your work with chocolate so much more fun, because you will get beautiful and durable results. The tempering only takes about 15 minutes.

Dark chocolate
temperature 1: 125°F (52°C)
temperature 2: 82°F (28°C)
temperature 3: 88°F (31°C)

Milk chocolate
temperature 1: 113°F (45°C)
temperature 2: 81°F (27°C)
temperature 3: 86°F (30°C)

White chocolate
temperature 1: 113°F (45°C)
temperature 2: 79°F (26°C)
temperature 3: 84°F (29°C)

You'll need a saucepan for the water, a stainless steel bowl (or use a double boiler), a candy thermometer, a rubber spatula, a knife—and of course the chocolate you're going to temper. The stainless steel bowl must have a larger circumference than the saucepan so that it hangs on the edge of the saucepan. The bowl must not touch the hot water.

1. Finely chop the chocolate.
2. Put one-third of the chocolate in a small bowl and the remaining two-thirds in the stainless steel bowl.
3. Put some water in the saucepan, making sure the water doesn't reach the stainless steel bowl, which will be placed above it later. Place the saucepan with water on the stove and bring the water almost to the boiling point. Remove the saucepan from the burner and place the stainless steel bowl over the water. Whatever you do, make sure you don't get water in the chocolate, or it will become lumpy. Remember that steam is water too! Gently stir with a thermometer. You don't want to stir in a lot of air. When the chocolate reaches temperature 1, remove the bowl from the saucepan.
4. Add the remaining ⅓ of the chocolate to the bowl and fold it in with a rubber spatula.
5. When the chocolate has melted, switch to the thermometer again instead of the spatula. Gently stir until the chocolate reaches temperature 2.
6. Put the bowl back on the saucepan. Now the chocolate is to be warmed back up to temperature 3. This will happen quickly. When it has reached the proper temperature, remove the bowl from the heat.
7. The chocolate is now ready to be used.

Save any leftover chocolate; it can be used again. You can either temper it again or use it in a cake.

ICING

An icing is mixed together in an instant and is the perfect departure point for all decorations. It can be used in so many ways. You can dip something in icing or cover whole surfaces with it. With the help of a piping bag, you can also draw whatever you want. You can add both flavor and color to your icing. You may have to make a few attempts in the beginning to get the right consistency. You simply have to acquaint yourself with the icing and the fact that various usages require different consistencies. Fortunately, you can easily adjust the consistency, whether you want a runnier or firmer icing.

Equipment
a small bowl
a spoon
a drinking glass (optional)
a piping bag (optional)

Main ingredients
icing sugar
egg white/water

Flavor suggestions
lemon juice/zest
lime juice/zest
orange juice/zest
rum extract
vanilla extract
mint extract
blueberry juice
raspberry juice
ground cardamom
cinnamon
ground ginger
vanilla
saffron
licorice root powder

liquid gel food coloring

1. Put the egg white or water in a small bowl, along with any liquid flavor you may be using. I often use 1 teaspoon of lemon juice in the icing to make it less sweet, but this is not necessary in order to make a beautiful icing. If you're using lemon juice, it's best to strain it. I almost exclusively make icing with egg white, which is harder and whiter than icing made from water. Sometimes I mix the icing sugar only with juice from citrus fruits or berries.
2. Add icing sugar and stir until you have a smooth mixture.
3. Add food coloring or spices (optional). The icing spots at the bottom of the page have added ginger, cinnamon, cardamom, and saffron. As you can see, the spices themselves add color in addition to flavor.
4. Is your icing too thick? Too thin? Adjust with liquid and icing sugar until you have the desired consistency. Test the consistency, and how the icing behaves, by lifting the spoon and allowing the icing to run off the spoon back into the bowl. You will then know if the icing is right for your purpose. At this point, the icing is done. Follow the next instructions if you're going to pipe it out.
5. Use either an ordinary freezer bag or a piping bag with a tip. Put a corner of the freezer bag or the tip of the piping bag into a glass and fold the bag over the rim. This will make it easier to fill the bag with icing.
6. Put the icing in the bag. You can tie the top of the bag if you want.
7. Cut a very small hole in the corner. If it turns out to be too small, it's easy to cut it some more. It's more difficult to make adjustments the other way around.
8. Pipe the icing either directly onto your baking or onto parchment paper. If you're making a shape with the icing, you can place a template under the parchment paper.

The remaining icing can be frozen. Freeze the entire bag. Then you can easily take it out and let it rest on the kitchen counter until it has defrosted and you're ready to use it.

1
2
3
4
5
6
7
8

MACARONS

makes 35 macarons

One of the best things about macarons is that the flavors of shells and fillings can be varied endlessly. The shapes and decorations also provide many possibilities. The macaron itself has a crisp shell with a moist inside and is easier and quicker to make than you might think.

Ingredients

¾ cup + 2 Tbsp (85 g) almond flour
¾ cup + 2 Tbsp (110 g) icing sugar
3 Tbsp (35 g) granulated sugar
2 medium egg whites (70 g)
pinch of salt
liquid gel food coloring (optional)
flavor (optional)

Macarons don't contain too many ingredients. Almond flour can be found in some stores' specialty sections. Use almond flour that hasn't been fat-reduced. Keep the eggs at room temperature beforehand. When you separate the whites from the yolks, it's very important that you don't get any yolk in the white. The yolk contains fat, and this will make it impossible to beat the meringue until it's thick.

Use liquid gel food coloring if you want to color the macarons. This type of food coloring won't change the consistency like liquid food coloring does. The macaron shells can also have flavor added in the form of spices, grated citrus zest, cocoa powder, etc.

Equipment

scale
2 mixing bowls
2 small bowls
electric hand mixer
sieve
rubber spatula
piping bag
macaron mat or parchment paper
(at least) 2 baking sheets
toothpicks

One of the mixing bowls and the handheld mixer must be completely free of grease. This is necessary in order to get a thick meringue. Some people suggest using a stainless steel bowl and removing the grease by rubbing it with a lemon, but I have always used a plastic bowl and just made sure to wash and dry it well.

I use a handheld electric mixer, but you can also use the balloon attachment on a kitchen stand mixer.

I use somewhat heavy disposable piping bags and cut a hole about ¼ inch (7 mm) in diameter to pipe out my macarons.

You'll need an extra baking sheet placed on the oven rack below the baking sheet with the macarons. This prevents the macarons from cracking.

Make the mixture

Sift the almond flour into a bowl. Stir in icing sugar and any spices you're using, then sift again into another bowl. Measure the granulated sugar into a small bowl. Using a handheld mixer or balloon attachment on a stand mixer, beat the egg white at medium speed until it is foamy. Add the salt. Gradually add the sugar, still beating at medium speed. When all the sugar has dissolved and you have a thick meringue, add color if you're using it. Add the almond flour mixture and use a rubber spatula to beat it into the meringue. Test if the meringue is ready by lifting some of the mixture with the rubber spatula and letting it drip into the bowl again. If the mixture is glossy and smooths itself out in the bowl, it's done.

Make the macaron shells

Put the mixture in a piping bag. Pipe out the macarons, either onto a macaron baking mat or parchment paper. If you need the help of a pattern when piping, you can draw the desired shape (see page 198) on a sheet of paper and put it under the parchment. You may want to fasten a piece of tape onto the regular paper, letting the tape extend beyond the parchment paper. Then you can easily pull out this sheet after you're finished piping, without disturbing the macarons. Tap the baking sheet with the macarons once against the kitchen counter so that any large air bubbles rise to the surface and burst. Use a toothpick to puncture the air bubbles that don't burst on their own.

Dry and bake the shells

If your oven has a convection setting, preheat it to 250°F (125°C). This will help the shells bake more quickly and evenly. If you don't have a convection setting, preheat the oven to 275°F (135°C) on the regular setting. Keep in mind that ovens bake differently, so you may have to adjust the temperature or the baking time. Place the extra baking sheet on the lower rack.

Let the macarons dry on the counter for about 40 minutes. Weather and temperature will affect the drying process; cold and humid weather will require a longer drying time.

Bake the macarons on the middle rack of the oven for about 15 minutes, or a few minutes longer if you're not using the convection setting. Remove from the oven and let the macarons cool on the baking sheet before you add the filling.

1
2
3
4
5
6

SPRINGFORM PAN TIPS

There are cake pans in all shapes and sizes. I most often use a springform pan with a diameter of 9 inches (23 cm). Here are some tips on getting an evenly baked cake that doesn't stick and has a flat top.

You will need
springform pan
parchment paper
scissors

To avoid having to grease and flour the pan, or cut a circle of parchment paper to fit perfectly in the bottom, you can do this:

1. Disassemble the springform pan.
2. Line the bottom of the pan with parchment paper and attach the bottom to the pan.
3. Cut around the edges.

---

terrycloth towel
scissors
safety pin

Cakes sometimes form a top in the middle while baking. It often happens because the cake is first baked along the outside edge, while the middle of the cake is still rising. You can easily fix this by wrapping a terrycloth towel around the pan while baking.

4. Cut a strip of a terrycloth towel. Make it the same width as the height of the springform pan. Make sure the strip is long enough to reach around the entire pan.
5. Soak the terrycloth in cold water and wring it out well.
6. Secure it around the springform pan with a safety pin. This strip of terrycloth can be used many times.

I often give the springform pan a little spin before I place it in the oven so the batter distributes itself evenly. It's typical to pour the batter into the middle of the pan, and then there's often more batter in the center than out toward the sides.

When the cake is done, loosen it from the sides and remove the springform. Place a wire baking rack, covered with a sheet of parchment paper, over the cake, and turn the whole thing over. The bottom of the cake is now at the top. Remove the parchment paper the cake was baked on. There are of course some cakes I don't flip—for example, the nut cake. Let the cake cool before it's sliced into layers and decorated, if that's your intention.

HOMEMADE CUPCAKE LINERS

Homemade cupcake liners are so cute. You can easily make your own from ordinary parchment paper. Place them in a muffin pan when you bake the cupcakes, or you'll have cupcake batter all over the oven.

You will need
parchment paper
cardboard/paper (optional)
scissors
drinking glass
muffin tray

1. Cut a square (about 5 inches/12 cm on each side) of cardboard or paper. You can use this as a template so you don't have to measure each subsequent piece.
2. Using the template, cut out parchment paper squares.
3. Take an ordinary drinking glass and turn it upside down.
4. Put the parchment square on top.
5. Put your hands on the parchment paper and pull it down along the sides of the glass. The parchment paper will take the shape of the glass.
6. Place the liner in a muffin pan. Make as many liners as you need.

Now, all you have to do is mix together the cupcake batter, fill the forms, and bake them.

1
2
3
4
5
6

RECIPE LIST

TEMPLATES

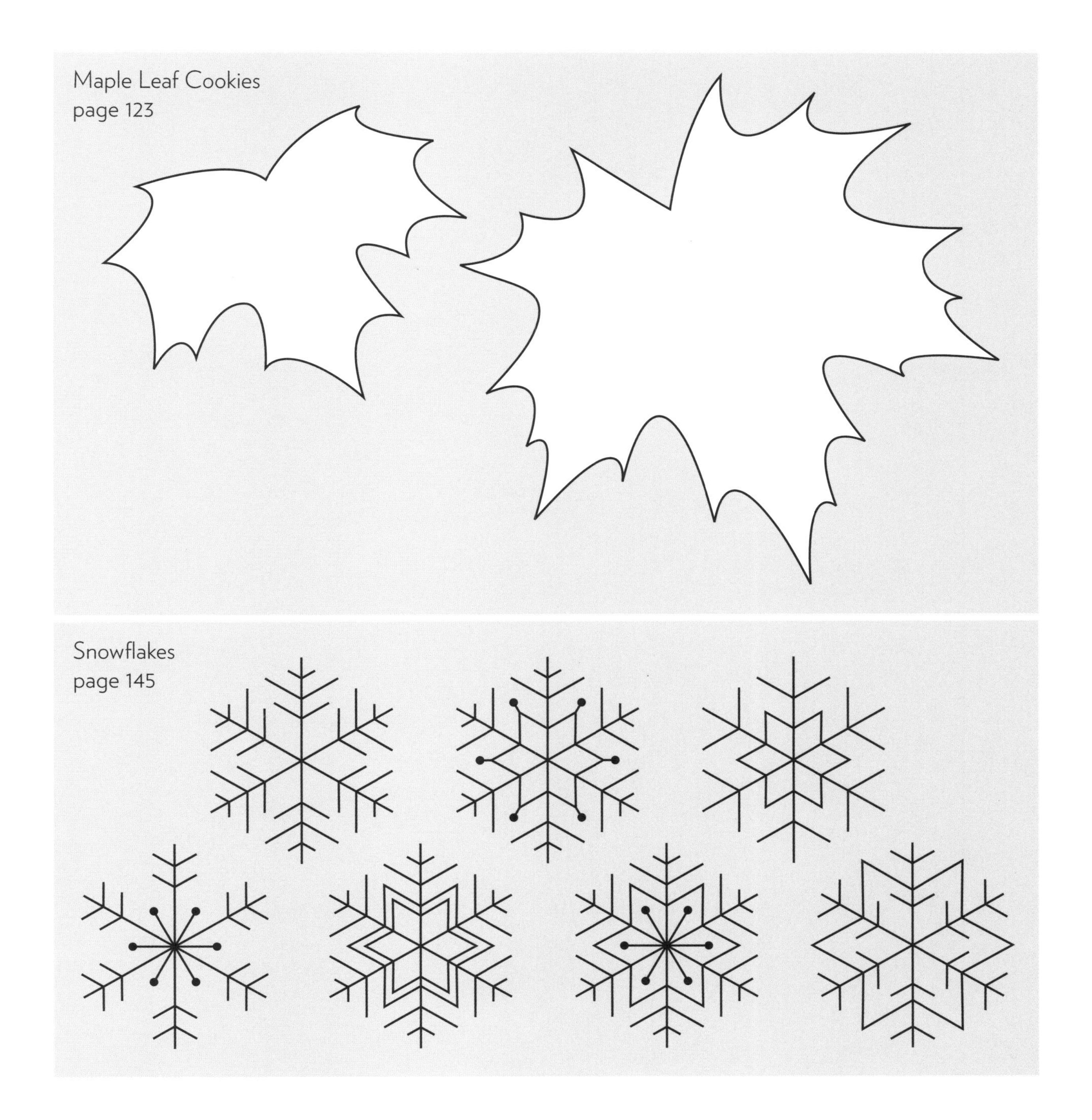

Brimstone Butterflies
page 51

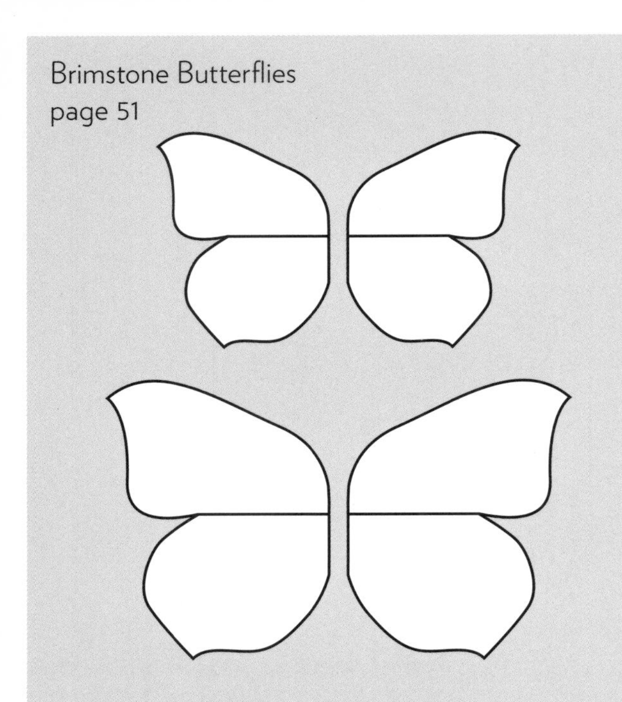

Snowflakes
page 145

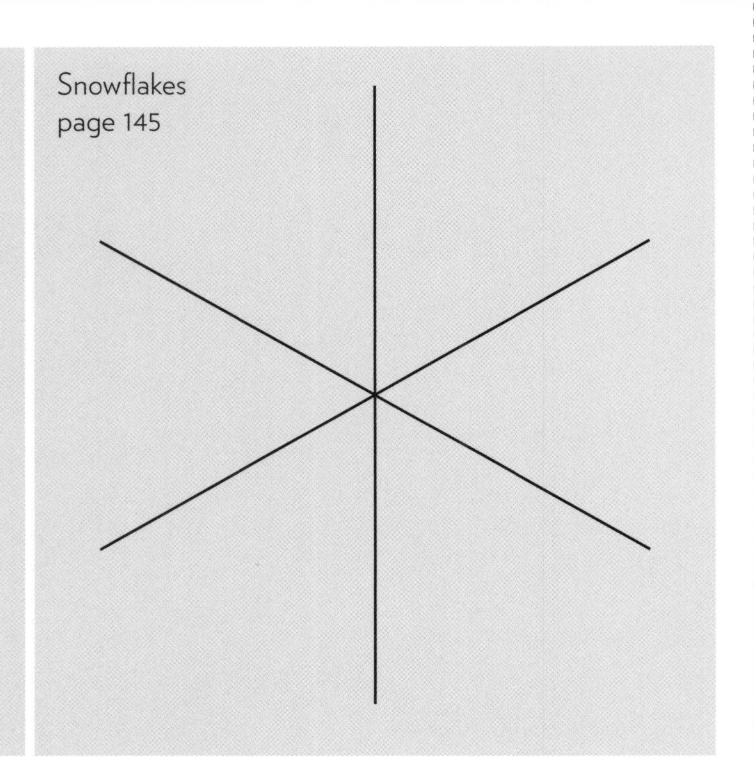

Blue Anemones
page 29

Birds' Eggs
page 25

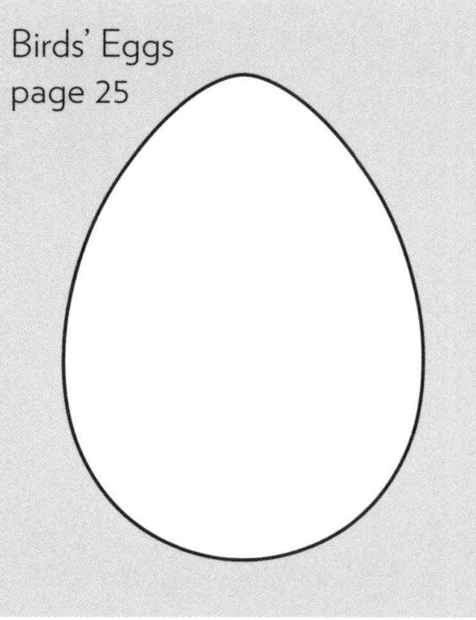

Strawberry Macaron
page 85

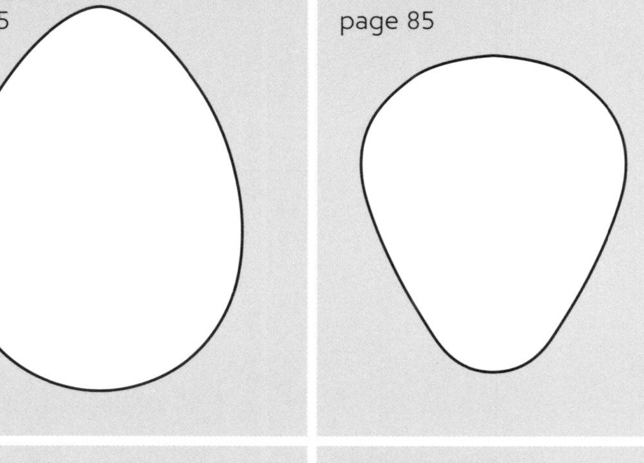

Buttercup
page 58

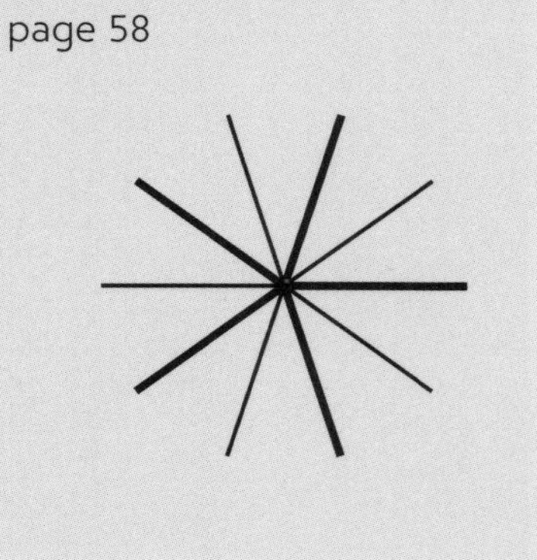

Macaron $1\frac{1}{4}$ inches
(3.5 cm)
pages 17, 85, 95, 103, 111, 142, 165, 190

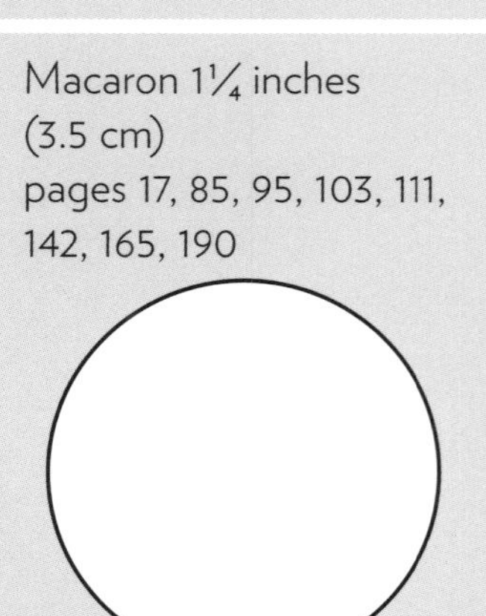

Icing Snowflakes
page 161

Norwegian Almond Cake Rings
page 151

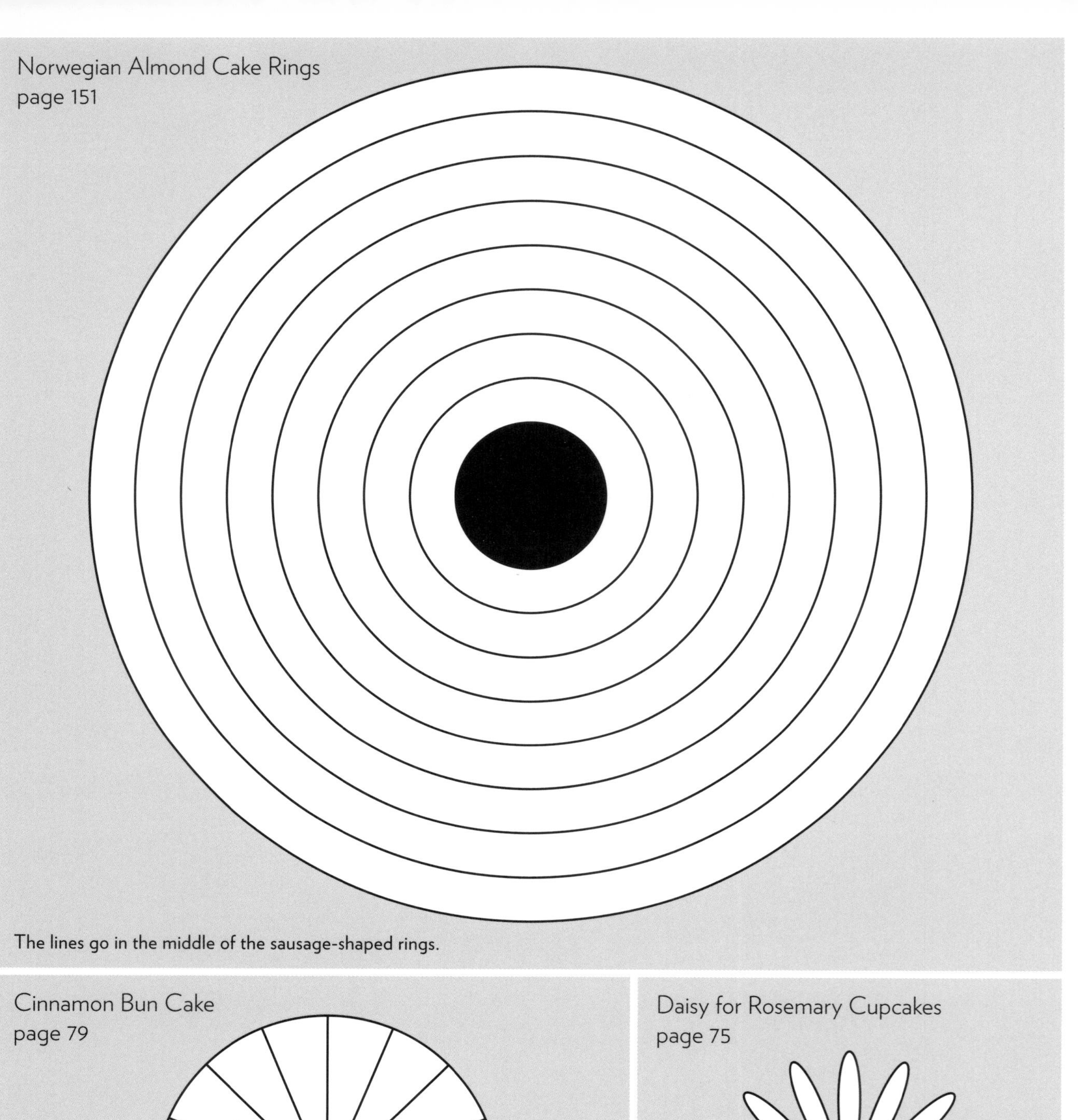

The lines go in the middle of the sausage-shaped rings.

Cinnamon Bun Cake
page 79

Daisy for Rosemary Cupcakes
page 75

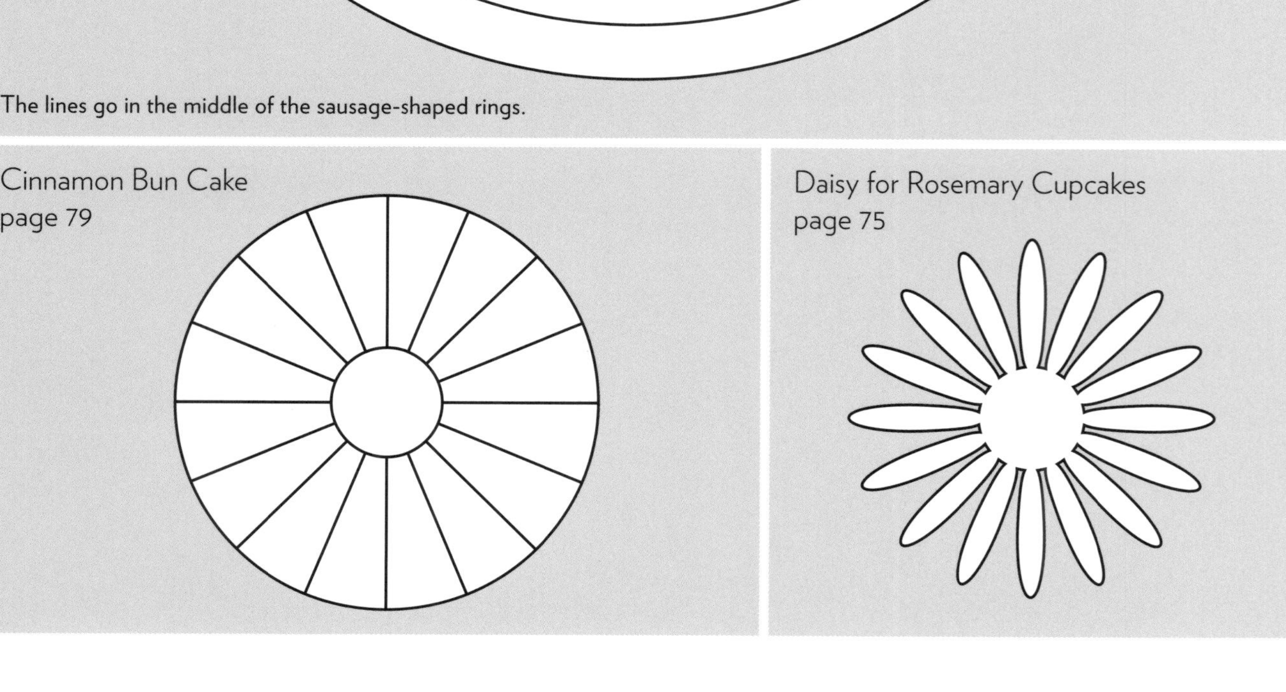

INDEX

Page numbers in italics refer to images

S

T

V

W

ABOUT

Marit Hovland is a graphic designer, photographer, and cookbook writer with a passion for baking and nature. She shares photos of her recipes, nature photography, and other hobbies on her website at borrowmyeyes.com, and with her more than 13,000 followers on Instagram at @borrowmyeyes. *Bakeland* is Marit's first book. She lives in Norway.

Trine Hahnemann is a Danish chef, food writer, and author of the internationally acclaimed *The Scandinavian Cookbook*, which has been translated into six languages. Her stories and recipes have appeared in the *Guardian*, *Fine Cooking US*, the *Observer Food Monthly*, *Good Housekeeping*, and many other publications.

18 19 20 21 22 5 4 3 2 1

Greystone Books Ltd.
www.greystonebooks.com

Cataloguing data available from Library and Archives Canada
isbn 978-1-77164-310-8 (cloth)
isbn 978-1-77164-311-5 (epub)

Copyedited by Paula Ayer
Cover design by Nayeli Jimenez
Interior design by Marit Hovland and Nayeli Jimenez
Cover photographs by Marit Hovland
Printed and bound in China on ancient-forest-friendly paper by 1010 Printing International Ltd.

We gratefully acknowledge the support of the Canada Council for the Arts, the British Columbia Arts Council, the Province of British Columbia through the Book Publishing Tax Credit, and the Government of Canada for our publishing activities.

Canadä